DRAMA CLASS

T0276709

The Drama Classics series
plays in affordable paperba__
and theatregoers. The hallmarks of the series are accessible
introductions, uncluttered texts and an overall theatrical
perspective.

Given that readers may be encountering a particular play for
the first time, the introduction seeks to fill in the theatrical/
historical background and to outline the chief themes rather
than concentrate on interpretational and textual analysis.
Similarly the play-texts themselves are free of footnotes and
other interpolations: instead there is an end-glossary of
'difficult' words and phrases.

The texts of the English-language plays in the series
have been prepared taking full account of all existing
scholarship. The foreign-language plays have been newly
translated into a modern English that is both actable and
accurate: many of the translators regularly have their work
staged professionally.

Edited until his early death by Kenneth McLeish, the Drama
Classics series continues with his aim of providing a first-class
library of dramatic literature representing the best of world
theatre.

Associate editors:
Professor Trevor R. Griffiths
Professor in Humanities, University of Exeter
Dr Colin Counsell
Senior Lecturer in Theatre Studies and Performing Arts

DRAMA CLASSICS *the first hundred*

The publishers welcome suggestions for further titles

DRAMA CLASSICS

THE GAME OF LOVE AND CHANCE

by

Pierre Marivaux

translated and introduced by
Stephen Mulrine

NICK HERN BOOKS
London
www.nickhernbooks.co.uk

A Drama Classic

The Game of Love and Chance first published in Great Britain in this translation as a paperback original in 2007 by Nick Hern Books Limited, The Glasshouse, 49a Goldhawk Road, London W12 8QP

Reprinted 2014

Copyright in the Introduction © 2007 Nick Hern Books Ltd
Copyright in this translation © 2007 Stephen Mulrine

Stephen Mulrine has asserted his right to be identified as the translator of this work

Typeset by Country Setting, Kingsdown, Kent CT14 8ES
Printed in Great Britain by Mimeo Ltd, Huntingdon, Cambs PE29 6XX

A CIP catalogue record for this book is available from the British Library

ISBN 978 1 85459 896 7

Woodland
CARBON
www.woodlandcarbon.co.uk
NICK HERN BOOKS
Printed on Carbon Captured paper

Introduction

Marivaux (1688–1763)

Pierre Carlet de Chamblain, later to adopt the *nom de plume* Marivaux, was born in Paris on 4 February 1688, the son of an army quartermaster, stationed in Germany. In 1698, his father purchased the office of Controller of the Royal Mint at Riom, in the Auvergne, becoming its Director in 1704, when the young Marivaux was able to join his father, whom he scarcely knew. Enrolled in law school in Paris in 1710, Marivaux neglected his studies in preference for literature, and in addition to publishing his first play, *A Father, Prudent and Just (Le Père prudent et équitable)* in 1712, also tried his hand at novel-writing – one titled, for example, *A Modern Don Quixote (Le Don Quichotte moderne)* – in the outmoded Spanish picaresque style. In the great literary dispute of the day, between the *Anciens,* faithful adherents to classical models, and the *Modernes,* propagandists for contemporary subjects and forms, Marivaux aligned himself firmly with the latter, going so far as to publish, in 1716, a burlesque of Homer's *Iliad,* signing his work 'Marivaux' for the first time.

In 1717, Marivaux married Colombe Bollogne, and in that same year began writing for the leading journal espousing the *Modernes'* cause, *Le Mercure,* with a series of articles on society modes and manners, *Lettres sur les habitants de Paris.* In 1719, his wife presented him with a daughter, Colombe-Prospère, an event unhappily overshadowed by the death of his father, not long after. At a time of intense financial speculation, which saw the infamous South Sea Bubble affair in England, the French equivalent, the Louisiana Company, set up by Scots banker John Law to further the development of the French territories in America, crashed spectacularly in 1720. The resultant casualties were widespread, and included Marivaux, who was compelled to resume his studies, receiving his licence to practise law the following year.

Marivaux continued to write, however, and found time to establish a new periodical, *Le Spectateur français*, a somewhat sporadic outlet for his journalism, inspired by the English *Spectator* of Addison and Steele. In March 1720, Marivaux also began a long association with the Théâtre Italien in Paris, and although his first comedy, *Love and Truth* (*L'Amour et la vérité*), was taken off after only one performance, the second, *Harlequin's Lesson in Love* (*Arlequin poli par l'amour*), in October of that year, was accounted a triumph. The same cannot be said for his only attempt at tragedy, a five-act verse play *Hannibal* (*Annibal*), which managed a mere three performances at the Comédie-Française in December. In general, the prevailing ethos of the latter, favouring strict classical verse and the heroic manner, was unsympathetic to Marivaux's talents, so the Italian actors became his chief interpreters.

After the death of his wife in 1723, leaving their five-year old daughter in his care, Marivaux never remarried, and Colombe-Prospère would eventually enter a convent, sponsored by the Duke of Orleans. Over the next few years, meanwhile, Marivaux succeeded in enhancing his reputation as a dramatist, through a series of productions with the Italian company – *The Surprise of Love* (*La Surprise de l'amour*);

Double Inconstancy (*La Double Inconstance*); and *The False Servant* (*La Fausse Suivante*) – though his next venture at the Comédie-Française, *The Unforeseen Outcome* (*Le Dénouement Imprévu*), was a relative failure. The culmination of this phase of Marivaux's dramatic career, *The Island of Slaves* (*L'Île des esclaves*), was premièred at the Théâtre Italien on 5 March, 1725, and became an instant success, managing some twenty performances, a long run by eighteenth-century standards, before being re-staged at the Court, and rapidly published. *The Island of Slaves* incidentally employs a plot device which Marivaux would return to five years later, in *The Game of Love and Chance* – that of master and valet, mistress and maidservant, changing places to their eventual benefit.

In 1726, Marivaux began work on his multi-volume novel *The Life of Marianne* (*La Vie de Marianne*), the publication of which would extend over almost ten years, and in March 1727, he founded another shortlived periodical, *The Indigent Philosopher* (*L'Indigent philosophe*). Later that same year, two new plays, *The Island of Reason* (*L'Île de la raison*), in September, and *The Second Surprise of Love* (*La Seconde surprise de l'amour*), in December, failed to make an impression at the Comédie-Française, and while the Théâtre Italien staged another Marivaux comedy, on the theme of Utopia, in 1729, little is known about *The New Colony* (*La Nouvelle colonie*), beyond a synopsis and a single act, published in 1750. However, Marivaux once again enjoyed a notable triumph, with the Théâtre Italien production of *The Game of Love and Chance* (*Le Jeu de l'amour et du hasard*), premièred in January 1730.

In company with such luminaries as Montesquieu and La Rochefoucauld, Marivaux was now a regular guest at all the fashionable Paris literary salons, including the twice-weekly soirées hosted by Madame de Lambert, one of a number of wealthy independent women who played an important role in forming the taste of the age. In 1734, Marivaux launched yet another periodical, *The Philosopher's Study* (*Le Cabinet du philosophe*), and that same year also saw the publication of the first two volumes of *The Life of Marianne*, along with a new novel, *The Upstart Peasant* (*Le Paysan parvenu*). Neither of these would ever be finished, but they are of considerable importance to the development of the genre in France. Meanwhile, despite the criticisms of Voltaire, who published an attack on him in *The Temple of Taste* (*Le Temple du goût*), Marivaux went on to consolidate his position as the country's leading dramatist, with a string of sparkling comedies throughout the next decade, including *The Triumph of Love* (*Le Triomphe de l'amour*); *The Rash Promises* (*Les Serments indiscrets*); *The Lucky Stratagem* (*L'Heureux stratagème*); *A Case of Mistaken Identity* (*La Méprise*); *The Fop Reformed* (*Le Petit-Maître corrigé*); *The False Confessions* (*Les Fausses confidences*); *Joy Unforeseen* (*La Joie imprévue*); and *The Test* (*L'Épreuve*). The latter, premièred in November 1740, was incidentally the last of his plays to be staged by the Théâtre Italien.

In 1742, Marivaux was elected to the Académie Française, ahead of Voltaire, and soon became one of its most active members, giving public lectures on a range of philosophical and literary topics. In 1744, however, the embarrassing failure of *A Matter of Dispute* (*La Dispute*) at the Comédie-Française, taken off after only one performance, somewhat dampened Marivaux's ardour for the theatre, and only a few more comedies would flow from his pen. Among these, *Victory over Prejudice* (*Le Préjugé vaincu*) managed a modest run at the Comédie-Française in 1746, and a new audience was found for some of his earlier works by the publication of a German translation in Hanover in 1747. Interestingly, in 1755, the Duke of Weimar took on the role of the shipwrecked master Iphicrate, compelled to change places with his servant, in a Court production of *The Island of Slaves*.

Though Marivaux continued dutifully to produce the occasional essay, or 'reflection', his final efforts for the theatre, including *The Faithful Wife* (*La Femme fidèle*), and *Actors in Good Faith* (*Les Acteurs de bonne foi*), were regrettably undervalued in his own lifetime, the last decade of which was marked by a steady decline in his fortunes, to such an extent that in his will, one of the few autobiographical documents he left behind, Marivaux confesses to having nothing to bequeath, apart from a small donation 'to the poor of this parish'. And even at the height of his fame, turning out one brilliant comedy, it seemed, after another, Marivaux laboured hard to win the respect his achievements in both the novel and drama merited, suffering the common fate of the artist ahead of his time. However, since his death in Paris, on 12 February 1763, Marivaux has come to be recognised as the greatest French playwright of the eighteenth century, and second only to Molière in the long and distinguished history of the theatre in France.

The Game of Love and Chance: ### What Happens in the Play

The action takes place throughout in a Paris drawing-room, and Act I opens with a young lady, Silvia, confessing her misgivings to her maid Lisette, about marriage in general, and her father's choice of suitor in particular, a certain

Dorante, whom she has never met, and who is expected at any moment. Lisette is unsympathetic, but with the approval of Orgon, Silvia's indulgent father, the maid consents to play her part in a ruse to discover Dorante's true character. This involves Silvia and Lisette changing places, but while they go off to swap clothes, Orgon reads Silvia's brother Mario a letter he has just received from Dorante's father, to the effect that Dorante has had exactly the same idea, and intends to change places with his valet. Orgon decides not to inform Silvia of this, but to let events run their course. Silvia then reappears dressed as her maidservant, and declares her intention to set her cap at Dorante, to test his steadfastness.

When Dorante arrives, in servant's livery, and calling himself Bourguignon, Orgon and Mario have some fun at the couple's expense, with Mario professing himself to be in love with the false 'Lisette'. Left alone, Silvia and Dorante, in the guise of their servants, then conduct a tentative courtship, ironically in the elevated style of their true high-born selves, until they are interrupted by the arrival of Dorante's valet Arlequin, who shocks Silvia/Lisette with his coarse demeanour, to the extent that Dorante is forced to rebuke his disguised valet in private, at the first opportunity. Orgon, for his part, naturally finds nothing to complain of in Arlequin/Dorante's behaviour, and makes him welcome.

At the beginning of Act II, Lisette warns Orgon that the 'false' Dorante appears to be attracted to her, and urges him to let Silvia reveal her true identity, before things get out of hand. Orgon tells Lisette that he would not object to her marrying Dorante, if the young man preferred the maidservant to her mistress, and goes on to quiz her on Silvia's opinion of Dorante's valet, Bourguignon. He then instructs Lisette to accuse Bourguignon of criticising his master behind his back. Next, Arlequin pays court to Lisette, until they are interrupted by Dorante/Bourguignon, who counsels his valet to exercise more restraint in his dealings with the 'false' Silvia. Heedless of his master's advice, Arlequin continues to declare his love for Lisette, who responds in kind. Unfortunately, the couple are again interrupted, this time by Silvia, who heatedly insists that Lisette is duty bound to discourage Arlequin, and is even more agitated when Lisette, obeying Orgon's instructions, is critical of Bourguignon.

Left alone, an indignant Silvia is only appeased by the arrival on the scene of Dorante, who throws caution to the winds and finally declares his love for her on bended knee, silently observed by Orgon and Mario. Silvia, in the guise of Lisette, is compelled to admit that she would still love 'Bourguignon', even supposing he were of noble birth. Orgon and Mario then reveal themselves and dismiss Dorante/Borguignon, accusing him of having disparaged his master. Silvia now decides to put an end to the whole charade, but her father refuses his permission, and she is further incensed by Mario's hints at her feelings towards Bourguignon. The latter, however, has also decided to end the pretence, and declares his true identity to the 'false' Lisette, with whom he is now deeply in love. Silvia is overjoyed, but continues to maintain her own disguise, and persuades her brother to assist her, by keeping up the pretence that he is still a rival for her affections.

In the opening scene of Act III, Arlequin pleads with his master to allow him to marry Lisette, whom they of course still believe to be Silvia. However, Dorante will only consent to this if Arlequin tells her the truth about his status. After Arlequin goes out, Mario appears, and deliberately tries to arouse Dorante's jealousy, as he has been instructed, by telling him that he is in love with 'Lisette', and has no desire to tolerate a rival, least of all a humble valet. Silvia/Lisette then enters, and Dorante demands to know what her relationship is with Mario; he receives no satisfaction, however, and Mario eventually orders him to leave. And when her father next appears, Silvia tells him of her latest scheme – to have Dorante ask for her hand while she is still in the guise of her maidservant. The real Lisette then enters, to ask Orgon for permission to marry the 'false' Dorante, which her master duly grants, on condition that she reveal her true identity. Lisette and Arlequin then engage in a comical exchange, at the end of which they confess to their mutual deception, and agree to keep the whole affair secret from Dorante a little while longer.

Dorante is astonished to hear that Silvia, as he imagines her to be, has consented to marry his valet, and moreover that her father is prepared to countenance their union, regardless of Arlequin's inferior status. As for himself, Dorante is gloomily convinced that he has no future with 'Lisette', and declares his intention to leave immediately, despite his love for her. Silvia responds to this with her own declaration of love, and Dorante joyfully asks for her hand in marriage. At this point, the happy couple are joined by Orgon and Mario, Lisette and Arlequin, in a final tableau, and only then, before the assembled company, does Silvia tell Dorante who she really is.

Marivaux and his Times

Marivaux wrote *Le Jeu de l'amour et du hasard* in 1729, during the reign of Louis XV, following the Regency of Philippe, Duke of Orleans, who had assumed the governance of France in 1715, after the death of Louis XIV. The twilight years of the 'Sun King' had been marked by widespread religious intolerance, periodic famine and epidemic, and an economy brought virtually to its knees by costly wars. A decade or so later, trade with America and the Orient was flourishing, and a rising class of merchants and entrepreneurs had begun to challenge an enfeebled nobility for supremacy. While Philippe restored many of the aristocrats' ancient rights and privileges, removed by his predecessor, the Regency period remained stagnant in political terms, its vital energies absorbed in pleasure-seeking, fuelled by the quick fortunes to be made through the Scots banker John Law's new paper money, which led to rampant inflation and catastrophic bank failure in 1720.

Louis XV came to the throne in 1723, inaugurating a period of peace and relative prosperity, mainly owing to improvements in industry and agriculture, which had a direct effect on life expectancy, resulting in a marked increase in population. The economy soon recovered from the Law fiasco, and commerce in general benefited from the new financial systems, though it must be said that the rising bourgeoisie were by far the chief beneficiaries. The social structure, however, remained rigidly hierarchical, with its tripartite division into clergy, nobility, and 'third estate'. The nobility, unable to engage in trade, and increasingly impoverished as a consequence, accounted for some 2% of the population, yet still enjoyed a position of dominance, soon to be challenged by the moneyed middle classes.

Marivaux exploits the tensions arising out of the rigid class system in a number of comedies, the best known being *The Island of Slaves* and *The Game of Love and Chance*, both of which employ the device of servants changing places with their masters or mistresses, occasioning some refined mockery of aristocratic manners, but it is significant that order is eventually restored, and the values of the *Ancien Régime* are never seriously questioned.

Marivaux's chief interest lies in the relationship between men and women, which had undergone something of a sea change within little more than a generation. Arranged marriages were no longer the inflexible rule, at least among the educated classes, and Marivaux's representation of an indulgent father, who is prepared to let his daughter pursue her own inclinations in choosing a husband, not only furnishes *The Game of Love and Chance* with its plot, but also reflects a genuine social trend. The spirit of the age, indeed, was to a considerable degree shaped by those powerful and independent women, whose hospitable drawing-rooms or *salons* had become a debating chamber for almost every artist of note, including Marivaux. It goes without saying that the topics of female emancipation, and the proper education of the modern woman, were high on the agenda, but the impact of *salon* culture on literary style, in the form of greater refinement, and more complex psychology, was also notable.

The importance of the *salon* to Marivaux's work cannot be over-estimated. Aside from its influence on his language, and his advanced views on the emancipation of women, Marivaux's stance in the protracted argument known as the *Querelle des Anciens et des Modernes* was also largely determined by his experiences in the *salon* of Madame de Lambert, where slavish adherence to classical models was routinely condemned in favour of originality, and contemporary French writing discussed as seriously as the works of Virgil or Homer.

Marivaux and the Theatre

Theatre was inevitably affected by these shifts in sensibility. Classical tragedy, hitherto the dominant mode, with its grandiose rhetoric and largely mythological content, was already losing ground, at the beginning of the eighteenth century, to drama derived from contemporary life, employing a more intimate language. Marivaux's own preferred genre was also changing, and the comedy of character, perfected by Molière, was steadily being supplemented, if not yet supplanted, by the comedy of sentiment, typically, in the work of Marivaux, expressed in the most refined and elegant prose, which his critics denigrated as wilfully obscure and precious, coining the pejorative term *marivaudage* to describe it. In a celebrated jibe, Voltaire said of Marivaux that he spent his days 'weighing flies' eggs on scales made from spider-webs'. Marivaux, however, insisted his work simply reflected the conversation of educated people – as indeed one imagines may have been the case, in the rarefied atmosphere of the Paris *salons*.

The *salon* ethos may also have played a part in Marivaux's recorded dislike of his great predecessor Molière, who more than once – notably in *The Pretentious Ladies* (*Les Précieuses ridicules*) and *The Learned Ladies* (*Les Femmes savantes*) – satirised the elegant circumlocutions of *préciosité*, and the affectation of its bluestocking exponents. *Le Misanthrope,* however, regarded by many as Molière's greatest play, occupies much common ground with Marivaux, both in refinement of language, and the sophistication of its relationships. But where Molière's comedy in general relies on stereotyped characters, whose excesses expose them to ridicule in a tightly organised plot, that of Marivaux, by contrast, is mostly concerned with analysis of the irrational nature of love – *la surprise de l'amour* – and is almost wholly dependent on dialogue, the spoken interplay of subtly shifting positions, as the characters respond to changes in their situation. Plot in fact plays a relatively minor role in all this, and once the basic conceit has been established in *The Game of Love and Chance,* the dramatic interest lies in observing how the two couples, each in the process of falling in love with the 'wrong' partner, attempt to reveal or conceal their true feelings or identities, as their relationship develops.

Silvia and Dorante, exchanging places with their servants independently, fall in love just as intended, their innate superiority shining through their disguises. To Silvia, the 'false' Dorante seems uncouth and repellent, while his earthy joviality soon wins over Lisette. The genuine Dorante, meanwhile, believes he has fallen in love with a lady's maid, and is about to give up in despair, before deciding to reveal his true identity. Silvia's instincts, she realises, have led her unerringly to her heart's desire, but in a neat twist, she resolves to keep her own identity secret still, to impel Dorante to the supreme sacrifice of proposing marriage to a servant, at the cost, if need be, of alienating his father. And with a few minor alterations, the same manoeuvres are comically duplicated between Arlequin and Lisette. The result is a narrative of fascinating complexity, in which the word, rather than the deed, is paramount.

In Marivaux's work, it has been said, all the action takes place in the mind. Equally noteworthy is the fact that Marivaux allows women far greater scope – even, as in *The Game of Love and Chance*, to assume the dominant role, in a manner hitherto unknown. Molière's Célimène, for example, albeit a complex and rounded creation, is nonetheless undoubtedly secondary to Alceste, the eponymous misanthrope. And in another important innovation, Marivaux subverts the traditional structure of comedy, by presenting us not with two lovers being kept apart by various obstacles, but with two people whose dramatic *raison d'être* is to *find* love, the more unexpectedly the better.

The Game of Love and Chance thus calls for actors, already by definition playing a part, to assume a secondary role, which *la surprise de l'amour*, against all their expectations, then invites them to abandon, in circumstances where they cannot do so openly. They are thus required to maintain the earlier fiction, as they attempt to respond truthfully to their new emotions, within the constraints of their disguises. The challenge this represents to the performer is immense: he or she is compelled to wear one mask, over which is superimposed another, without entirely concealing the first – as the speech and manner, despite their best efforts, of master/valet, mistress/maid tend to make clear. Linked to this, the question of who knows what, and when they become aware of it, or choose to admit it, even to themselves, imposes an additional burden on the actor, and it is in these tensions, teased out with consummate artistry, that Marivaux finds his dramatic interest, while the audience in turn, from a position of superior knowledge, enjoys the familiar theatrical experience of dramatic irony.

However, although the question of the mask, and its necessary function in human intercourse, has a clear modern appeal, Marivaux's apparent conviction that true nobility of spirit, which cannot be disguised, is somehow imprinted in the genetic inheritance of the Dorantes of this world, and never to be found in the coarse-grained lower orders, regardless of their other virtues, is less engaging – evidence, if any were needed, of how deeply ingrained the hierarchy of social class was in the France of Marivaux's day. Significantly, Marivaux avoids placing the real Arlequin and Silvia in dialogue together, which would have been a serious breach of decorum, and contemporary criticism of the play takes issue with just that shocking proposition.

In other respects, Marivaux is remarkably modern – the recurrent theme in his work of the deceptive character of reality nowadays finds a ready response. And while the concept of a play within the play is by no means Marivaux's invention, the degree of sophistication he brings to the device in, for example, *Actors in Good Faith* (*Les Acteurs de bonne foi*), a one-act comedy published in 1757, but unperformed, even anticipates Pirandello in the 1920s.

The Game of Love and Chance on Stage

In all, Marivaux wrote some forty plays, the majority of which were staged by the Théâtre Italien, the inheritors of that *commedia dell'arte* tradition so much admired and imitated by Molière. Though the original Italian company had been expelled from France in 1697, they were invited to return, following the death of Louis XIV, by the Duke of Orleans, and took up residence again in the Hôtel de Bourgogne in 1716, ready and waiting, as it were, to receive Marivaux's work. In contrast to the Comédie-Française, whose declamatory performing style was essentially unsuited to Marivaux, and where he enjoyed only modest success, the legacy of the *commedia dell'arte*, with its familiar stock characters and loosely improvised dialogue, made the Italian actors the perfect interpreters of Marivaux. From 1720 onwards, beginning with *Harlequin's Lesson in Love* (*Arlequin poli par l'amour*), his first play written for the company, one triumph followed another, and *The Game of Love and Chance* was the tenth Marivaux play to be premièred by the Théâtre Italien.

In general, the Italian actors played the same stock characters from one play to the next, and the names Marivaux assigns to the *dramatis personae* of *The Game of Love and Chance* – Arlequin, Dorante, Mario, Silvia, and so on – are adopted unchanged from the Italian repertoire, and recur throughout his work. Arlequin, for example, who figures in most of Marivaux's comedies, was routinely performed by an actor known as Thomassin, much admired for the subtlety he had brought to a traditionally rather knockabout role, and duly rewarded, in *The Game of Love and Chance*, by elevation to the status of second lover. Likewise the celebrated actress Gianetta Rosa Benozzi, who played all of Marivaux's many Silvias, over a period of two decades, was able to explore every nuance of a character fitted to her like a second skin. Accordingly, *The Game of Love and Chance* was well received at its première in January 1730, with a first run of fifteen performances at the Théâtre Italien, followed by Versailles, and a revival in December of that same year. Unfortunately, as old age caught up with Marivaux's gifted interpreters, so his reputation declined, and the Théâtre Italien itself merged with the Opéra Comique in 1762, shortly before the playwright's own death.

Performances of Marivaux's work thereafter rapidly dwindled, as the political climate in the latter part of the century became increasingly unsympathetic to his moderate reform agenda, and cultivated graciousness. *Marivaudage* was already employed as a pejorative term, suggestive of frivolous logic-chopping, and the situation improved only marginally over the next century, when a mere handful of Marivaux's plays, *The Game of Love and Chance* among them, continued to be performed at the Comédie-Française. Following some groundbreaking scholarship in the twentieth century, however, Marivaux steadily returned to favour, aided by several noteworthy French productions, including *Les fausses confidences* (1946), by Jean-Louis Barrault, and *La Seconde surprise de l'amour* (1953), by Roger Planchon. Jean-Paul Roussillon's 1976 staging of *The Game of Love and Chance* at the Comédie Française was also widely praised, while more recently, Alfredo Arias's 1986 production of the same play for Théâtre TSE aroused controversy with its extraordinary device of presenting the characters as apes! By conventional measurement, however, Marivaux's current status is shown by the fact that some three-quarters of his plays are now in the repertoire of the Comédie-Française, with *The Game of Love and Chance* most popular, judged by number of performances (1600-odd by 1996), followed by *La Commère* and *Le Triomphe de l'amour.* Molière, of course, heads the all-time list, with three times the number of productions of his closest rival, Racine, but Marivaux comes a creditable fifth, behind Corneille and Musset. And in an intriguing modern twist, proving the play's staying power, *The Game of Love and Chance* has recently been adapted for the screen as *L'Esquive,* by the Tunisian director Abdellatif Kechiche, centred on a group of teenagers in a Paris housing scheme, taking part in a school production of the Marivaux classic, which spills over into their own lives.

Le Jeu de l'amour at du hasard was translated into English as early as 1735, by Lady Mary Wortley-Montagu, but her version, titled *Simplicity,* was not staged in England until 1988, although it was successfully revived in October 2003 at the Orange Tree, Richmond, directed by Auriol Smith. Prior to that, *The Game of Love and Chance,* in a version by John Walters, directed by Robert Cordier, was premièred at the Nuffield Theatre, Southampton, in February 1986. Interestingly, the first reported staging of *The Game of Love and Chance* in New York was as recent as November 1993, by the Pearl Theater. And on 12 January that same year, the Royal National Theatre, in a co-production with the Cambridge Theatre Company, staged the play at the Cottesloe in Neil Bartlett's adaptation, directed by Mike Alfreds.

Marivaux: Key Dates

1688   Born Pierre Carlet de Chamblain in Paris, 4
       February.
1698   Father Nicolas appointed to head Royal Mint at
       Rion, in the Auvergne.
1710   Marivaux enters Faculty of Law in Paris.
1712   Verse play, *A Father Prudent and Just* (*Le Père prudent et
       equitable*) for amateur theatre in Limoges.
1716   Verse parody of Homer, *L'Iliade travestie*, signed
       'Marivaux' for first time.
1717   Marries Colombe Bollogne. Essays, *Lettres sur les
       habitants de Paris*.
1719   Birth of daughter, Colombe-Prospère; 14 April,
       death of father.
1720   Collapse of Louisiana Company, rendering
       Marivaux bankrupt. 3 March, *Love and Truth*
       (*L'Amour et la vérité*), Théâtre Italien; 17 October,
       Harlequin's Lesson in Love (*Arlequin poli par l'amour*),
       Théâtre Italien; 16 December, *Hannibal* (*Annibal*),
       Comédie-Française.
1721   20 June, obtains licence to practise law.
1722   3 May, *The Surprise of Love* (*La Surprise de l'amour*),
       Théâtre Italien.
1723   6 April, *Double Inconstancy* (*La Double inconstance*),
       Théâtre Italien. Death of Marivaux's wife.
1724   5 February, *The Prince in Disguise* (*Le Prince travesti*),
       Théâtre Italien; 8 July, *La Fausse suivante* (*The False*

Servant*), Théâtre Italien; 2 December, *The Unforeseen Outcome* (*Le Dénouement imprévu*), Comédie-Française.

1725   5 March, *The Island of Slaves* (*L'Île des esclaves*), Théâtre Italien; 19 August, *The Farmer Inherits a Fortune* (*L'Héritier du village*), Théâtre Italien.

1727   11 September, *The Island of Reason* (*L'Île de la raison*), Comédie-Française; 31 December, *The Second Surprise of Love* (*La Seconde surprise de l'amour*), Comédie-Française.

1728   22 April, *Plutus Triumphant* (*Le Triomphe de Plutus*), Théâtre Italien.

1729   18 June, *The New Colony* (*La Nouvelle colonie*), Théâtre Italien.

1730   23 January, *The Game of Love and Chance* (*Le Jeu de l'amour et du hasard*), Théâtre Italien.

1731   *The Life of Marianne* (*La Vie de Marianne*), novel; Part I ; 5 November, *Two Loves Reconciled* (*La Réunion des amours*), Théâtre Italien.

1732   12 March, *The Triumph of Love* (*Le Triomphe de l'amour*), Théâtre Italien; 8 June, *The Rash Promises* (*Les Serments indiscrets*), Comédie-Française; 25 July, *The School for Mothers* (*L'École des mères*), Théâtre Italien.

1733   6 June, *The Lucky Stratagem* (*L'Heureux stratagème*, Théâtre Italien.

1734   *The Life of Marianne*, Part II; *The Upstart Peasant* (*Le Paysan parvenu*), novel, Parts I-IV; 16 August, *A Case of Mistaken Identity* (*La Méprise*), Théâtre Italien.; 6 November, *The Fop Reformed* (*Le Petit-Maître corrigé*), Comédie-Française.

1735   9 May, *The Confidante Mother* (*La Mère confidente*), Théâtre Italien; *The Life of Marianne*, Part III.

1736   *The Life of Marianne*, Parts IV-VI.

1737   *The Life of Marianne*, Part VII; *The Inheritance (Le Legs)*, Comédie-Française; 16 March, *False Confessions (Les Fausses confidences)*, Théâtre Italien.

1738   *The Life of Marianne*, Part VIII; 7 July, *Joy Unforeseen (La Joie imprévue)*, Théâtre Italien.

1739   13 January, *Sincerity (Les Sincères)*, Théâtre Italien.

1740   19 November, *The Test (L'Epreuve)*, Théâtre Italien.

1741   *The Gossip (La Commère)*, Théâtre Italien, unperformed.

1742   *The Life of Marianne*, Parts IX-XI.

1743   4 February, Marivaux elected to Académie Française.

1744   19 October, *A Matter of Dispute (La Dispute)*, Comédie-Française.

1745   Daughter Colombe-Prospère enters convent.

1746   6 August, *Victory over Prejudice (Le Préjugé vaincu)*, Comédie-Française.

1750   *The Colony (La Colonie)*, for private theatre of Comte de Clermont.

1755   24 August, *The Faithful Wife (La Femme fidèle)*, Théâtre de Berny.

1757   5 March, *Félicie*, published in *Le Mercure*; November, *Actors in Good Faith (Les Acteurs de bonne foi)*, published in *Le Conservateur*.

1761   *The Country Wife (La Provinciale)*, published in *Le Mercure*.

1763   12 February, after lengthy illness, Marivaux dies in rue Richelieu, Paris.

For Further Reading

The basic raw materials of biography – letters, diaries, etc. – are extremely scant in the case of Marivaux, and very little is known about his private life, apart from what can be gleaned from official documents. There are accordingly few accounts of his life, in French or English, but *Marivaux*, by Oscar A. Haac, in the Twayne's World Authors series (TWAS 294), New York, 1974, is useful, with detailed synopses of his work, and a handy bibliography. Easier to obtain is the Bristol Classical Press *Marivaux: Le Jeu de l'amour et du hasard*, edited by D.J. Culpin, and published by Gerald Duckworth & Co., 2005, which introduces the French text of the play with extensive commentary and analysis, and an updated bibliography. For the wider context, W.D. Howarth's compilation of original documents, *French Theatre in the Neo-Classical Era, 1550-1789*, published by Cambridge University Press, 1997, is also valuable.

Other scholarly resources include Donald C. Spinelli's *Concordance to Marivaux's Comedies in Prose*, in four volumes, published by the University of North Carolina, 1979; E.J.H. Greene's history of Marivaux criticism, *Marivaux*, Toronto University Press,1965; George Poe's *The Rococo and Eighteenth Century French Literature: a Study through the Theatre of Marivaux*, published by Peter Lang, New York, 1987; D.J. Culpin's *Marivaux and Reason*, for the same publisher,1997; and V.P. Brady's *Love in the Theatre of Marivaux*, Droz, Geneva, 1970.

THE GAME OF LOVE AND CHANCE

Characters

ORGON

MARIO

SILVIA

DORANTE

LISETTE, *Silvia's maid*

ARLEQUIN, *Dorante's valet*

A LACKEY

The scene is set in Paris.

ACT ONE

SILVIA, LISETTE.

SILVIA. I'm asking you again – what business is it of yours? What gives you the right to offer an opinion on my feelings?

LISETTE. Well, I just assumed that in a situation like this, your feelings would be the same as anybody else's. Your father asks me if you're quite happy that he's marrying you off – if you're pleased about it. So I tell him yes, of course you are. Now, you may be the only girl in the world for whom that 'yes' isn't true, but 'no' – well, it's just not natural.

SILVIA. So 'no' isn't natural? What a stupid thing to say! Marriage really does appeal to you, does it?

LISETTE. Well, I'd still say yes, I'll tell you that.

SILVIA. Oh, be quiet – take your impertinent nonsense off elsewhere, and don't even think of judging my heart by your own.

LISETTE. My heart's the same as everybody else's. Where does yours get the idea that it's so different from other people's?

SILVIA. Honestly, she'd call me a freak, if she had the nerve!

LISETTE. If I were your equal, we'd soon see.

SILVIA. You're deliberately annoying me, Lisette.

LISETTE. Well, I don't mean to, but when you come right down to it, what harm did I do telling Monsieur Orgon that you were quite happy about getting married?

SILVIA. For a start, that's simply not true – I'm actually quite content to be a spinster.

LISETTE. Now, that's another one I haven't heard before.

SILVIA. So my father needn't think he's doing me such a great favour marrying me off. And you'll only give him the confidence to go ahead now, and no doubt waste his time.

LISETTE. What, you mean you won't marry the man he's picked out for you?

SILVIA. How do I know? Quite possibly he won't appeal to me at all, and that worries me.

LISETTE. Well, people say your future husband is a very fine gentleman – he's tall and good-looking, good-humoured, too. He's also extremely clever, and you couldn't ask for a better person – what more do you want? Can you imagine a more delightful union? A marriage made in heaven, I'd say.

SILVIA. Made in heaven! Really, you and your silly expressions!

LISETTE. Believe me, ma'am, you're very lucky a man like that is prepared to go the length of a proper ceremony. If he were to set his cap at a girl, there's scarcely one who wouldn't be in danger of marrying him without a blessing, if you know what I mean. He's charming and handsome – positively made for love. Besides which, he's good company, and witty – just perfect for society. Heavens above, the man must be a good catch, surely? Useful and agreeable, too – he's got everything.

SILVIA. Yes, that's the picture you paint of him, and people say it's a good likeness. But that's just hearsay, and I might not share that view. He *is* good-looking, by all accounts, but I'm more inclined to say worse luck.

LISETTE. Worse luck? Worse luck? Now, there's a bizarre notion!

SILVIA. Not at all – it's entirely sensible. Handsome men, I've noticed, tend to be conceited.

LISETTE. Well, he's wrong to be conceited, but he's within his rights to be handsome.

SILVIA. They also say he's tall and well-built, but we'll let that pass.

LISETTE. Oh yes, we can forgive him for that!

SILVIA. I mean, handsome, good-looking – these are luxuries I can dispense with.

LISETTE. Good God! If I ever get married, they'll be necessities!

SILVIA. You don't know what you're saying. In marriage it's generally the rational man you have to deal with, not the lover. In a word, all I ask of him is a kind heart, and that's harder to find than people think. Everyone speaks highly of his, but who has actually lived with him? Yes, men are rather good at projecting a false image of themselves, particularly the clever ones. I've seen more than a few myself, who seemed to be the nicest people you could meet, all sweet reason and bonhomie – in company, that is. Oh yes, their sterling qualities were guaranteed by their very faces, or so you would think. 'Monsieur So-and-so seems a real gentleman, so polite and thoughtful.' That's what they used to say all the time about Ergaste. 'Oh, absolutely!' others would say –

indeed, I've said it myself – 'A face like that couldn't possibly lie.' Well, let me tell you, that gentle exterior, so kind and considerate, disappears a quarter of an hour later, to be replaced by a grim countenance – fierce and brutal enough to terrify an entire household! Ergaste got married, and the only face his wife and children, and the servants, ever see, is that dark, brooding scowl. Meanwhile, he parades his other face, the one we all know, that amiable façade, to the world outside, like a mask he puts on whenever he leaves the house.

LISETTE. He must be a very strange person, to have two faces!

SILVIA. And aren't people always happy to see Léandre? Well, at home he never utters a word, he doesn't laugh, he doesn't even complain. He's a cold fish – completely soulless and quite unapproachable. His wife doesn't know him at all, she has no communication with him. She's married to a sort of apparition, who emerges from his study at meal-times, only to put a damper on the whole company, with his cold-blooded apathy and listlessness. Now, how's that for an amusing husband?

LISETTE. That makes *my* blood run cold. Well, what about Tersandre, then?

SILVIA. Oh yes, Tersandre. He'd flown into a rage with his wife the other day, just before I called on them. And when I'm announced, I see a man coming towards me with open arms, so calm and relaxed you would swear he'd just been having the most amiable conversation – the hint of laughter still playing around his eyes and mouth. Such deceit! Well, that's what men are like. And who would believe that his wife had anything to complain about? When I went in I found her utterly miserable, pale as death, and her eyes still red from weeping – exactly the way I might be, my future portrait, perhaps. Well, I'm not going to risk becoming a copy. I felt very sorry for her, Lisette – and suppose I were to make you sorry for me? It's a terrible thought, don't you agree? Think about it – what *is* a husband?

LISETTE. A husband? Well, it's a husband, isn't it? You know, you shouldn't have ended with that word, it makes all the rest seem bearable!

Enter ORGON.

ORGON. Ah, good morning, my dear. I've just received some news, which I'm sure will please you. Your future husband is arriving today – I have a letter here from his father. What, you've nothing to say, and you look unhappy? And Lisette lowers her eyes – what does this mean? Lisette, tell me – what's the matter?

LISETTE. Oh, sir – a face that would make you shiver, another that would freeze your blood, a real cold fish, with no soul, and then the portrait of a woman looking absolutely miserable, pale as death, her eyes all puffy from weeping. That's what we've been discussing.

ORGON. What's all this nonsense? Souls, portraits – explain yourself. I haven't a clue what you're on about.

SILVIA. I've just been talking to Lisette about unhappy wives, mistreated by their husbands, and I mentioned Tersandre's wife, whom I found the other day terribly depressed, because he'd picked a quarrel with her, and I was making a few observations on the subject.

LISETTE. Yes, we were talking about people with two faces – husbands who wear a mask for the outside world, and a permanent scowl at home.

ORGON. From which, my dear girl, I gather you're a little uneasy about this marriage – the more so since you don't know Dorante at all.

LISETTE. Well, to start with, he's very good-looking – worse luck.

ORGON. Worse luck? Have you gone mad?

LISETTE. I'm only repeating what I've learned. This is my lady's teaching, I'm just her pupil.

ORGON. Oh, come, this is absurd. My dear child, you know how much I love you. Dorante is coming here to marry you. On my last trip to the provinces, I arranged this marriage with his father, who is my oldest and closest friend, but it was all on condition that you liked each other, and you would have complete freedom to discuss the matter. I absolutely forbid you to do anything just to please me. If Dorante isn't to your liking, you have only to say so, and he'll be gone. And the same applies if you don't appeal to him.

LISETTE. Yes, it'll all be decided through a love-duet, like at the opera: You want me, I want you, quick, send for a lawyer! Either that, or it's: Do you love me? No. I don't love you either. Quick, saddle up!

ORGON. Actually, I've never seen this Dorante – he was away somewhere when I was at his father's house. But from everything I've been told, I've very little fear that either of you will be in a hurry to say goodbye.

SILVIA. I truly appreciate your kindness, father – you've forbidden me to do anything just to please you, and that I shall obey.

ORGON. I insist on it!

SILVIA. But if I may be so bold, I have a suggestion to make – an idea that's just come to me – and if you'd grant me this favour, it would really set my mind at rest . . .

ORGON. Tell me, and if it's at all possible, I'll do it.

SILVIA. Oh, it's certainly possible, but I'm afraid I may be abusing your good nature.

ORGON. Go right ahead, abuse it. Too kind's seldom kind enough, in this world of ours.

LISETTE. Only the very best of men would say a thing like that.

ORGON. Go on, tell me, my dear.

SILVIA. Well, Dorante is coming here today. Now, what if I could observe him, give him the once-over without him knowing who I was? Lisette's pretty clever, she could take my place for a short while, and I could take hers.

ORGON (*aside*). That's rather an amusing idea. (*Aloud.*) Let me give it some thought a moment. (*Aside.*) If I allow her to do it, something strange is bound to happen – something she's not expecting herself . . . (*Aloud.*) Very well, my dear, I'll permit this disguise. Are you sure you can play your part, Lisette?

LISETTE. Me, sir? Well, you know what I'm like . . . 'Just try to take advantage of me, or show me a lack of respect, if you dare!' There – that's an example of the expression I'll put on, the fine airs and graces I'll receive you with. What do you think, eh? Can you still see Lisette?

ORGON. Good heavens, no – you've actually managed to fool me! Now, there's no time to lose. Go and get dressed to play your new part. Dorante might arrive any minute, so hurry – and make sure all the other servants are in on it.

SILVIA. All I need is an apron.

LISETTE. Well, I'm having the full works – come on, Lisette, you'll have to do my hair now, you'd better get used to your duties. And take a little more care, too, if you please.

SILVIA. I'll do my best, your ladyship. Now, let's go!

Enter MARIO.

MARIO. My dear sister, congratulations! I've just heard the news, and I gather we're to see your beloved?

SILVIA. Indeed yes, dear brother, but I can't stop – I've got some serious business to attend to. Father will explain. Goodbye for now.

Exeunt SILVIA *and* LISETTE.

ORGON. Don't detain her, Mario. Come and I'll let you know you what it's about.

MARIO. What's going on, sir?

ORGON. Well, let me start by warning you to be discreet about what I'm going to tell you.

MARIO. I'll do whatever you say.

ORGON. We're going to see Dorante today, but we'll be seeing him in disguise.

MARIO. Disguise? In fancy dress, do you mean – are you giving a masked ball?

ORGON. Let me read you part of this letter I've received from his father. Mmm . . . 'I don't know what you will think of this strange notion my son has conceived. It really is most peculiar, as he himself agrees, but his motives are understandable, and quite subtle, I suppose.

He has asked me to permit him to arrive at your home first in disguise as his own valet, who in turn will play the part of his master . . . '

MARIO. That ought to be fun.

ORGON. Listen to the rest . . . 'My son realises how serious is the step which he is about to take, and hopes, so he says, to employ this brief period of disguise to discover something of the true nature of our young bride-to-be, and to get to know her better, so that he can more easily decide what to do, in light of the freedom of choice we have agreed to permit them. For my part, trusting in everything you have told me about your charming daughter, I have given my consent, but I am taking the precaution of informing you, although he did ask me to keep it secret from you. As far as the bride-to-be is concerned, you must act as you see fit . . . ' Now, that's what his father writes to me, but there's more to it. Your sister is anxious about Dorante on her own account, and although she doesn't know his secret, she has asked my permission to play the same game, precisely in order to observe Dorante, as he wishes to observe her! Now, what do you think of that? Have you ever heard the like? Mistress and maid are changing places this very minute. What should I do, Mario? Should I tell your sister or not?

MARIO. Good heavens no, father. If that's the way things are headed, I wouldn't interfere with them. They've both been inspired by the same idea, and I would respect that. They should be encouraged to meet and talk often, in these disguises. Then let's see if their hearts won't alert them as to their true worth. Possibly Dorante will take a fancy to my sister even though she's a maidservant, which would be delightful for her.

ORGON. Well, we'll see how she gets herself out of this predicament.

MARIO. Anyway, it can't fail to be a most amusing business altogether, and I want to be there right from the start, to jolly the pair along.

Enter SILVIA.

SILVIA. Now, here I am – I don't look too bad as a chambermaid, do I? And you, my dear brother – I assume you know what's afoot – how do you find me?

MARIO. Frankly, dear sister, the valet is as good as yours, and you could quite easily steal Dorante himself from your mistress to boot.

SILVIA. To be honest, I wouldn't be averse to attracting him in this part I'm playing. No, indeed, I rather fancy turning his head, and trying to make him forget the gulf that separates us socially. If my charms can accomplish that feat, I'll be well pleased with myself. Besides which, it'll help me get a true picture of Dorante. As for his valet, I've no fear of him. Let him sigh all he likes, he won't make any advances, he wouldn't dare. There'll be something about my demeanour which will invite respect, rather than love, from that rascal.

MARIO. Not so fast, dear sister – that so-called rascal will be your equal.

ORGON. And he's bound to fall in love with you.

SILVIA. Fine, that honour will come in very handy. Valets are by nature indiscreet, and love loosens the tongue, so I'll make him tell tales on his master.

Enter VALET.

VALET. Sir, there's a servant outside, asking to speak to you. And there's a porter with him carrying some luggage.

ORGON. Send him in. It'll be Dorante's valet. No doubt his master has stopped off at the freight office, to attend to some business or other. Now, where's Lisette?

SILVIA. Lisette's getting dressed, admiring herself in the mirror. She now thinks it's decidedly foolish of us, handing Dorante over to her, but she won't be long.

ORGON. Ssshh! Someone's coming.

Enter DORANTE, *dressed as a valet.*

DORANTE (*bows*). I am looking for Monsieur Orgon – is it not himself to whom I have the honour of paying my respects?

ORGON. It is indeed himself, my friend.

DORANTE. Sir, you have doubtless received word of our coming. I am in Monsieur Dorante's service. My master, who will be arriving shortly, has sent me on ahead to assure you of his best respects, until he can do so in person.

ORGON. And you have performed your errand most graciously. Lisette, what do you say of this young man?

SILVIA. I say he is most welcome, sir, and that he shows promise.

DORANTE. You are very kind. I do my best.

MARIO. He's not bad-looking, at any rate – you'd better watch out for your heart, Lisette.

SILVIA. My heart? What's all this nonsense?

DORANTE. Don't be angry, mam'selle. Whatever the gentleman said, I've no illusions on that score.

SILVIA. Good, I like that. Modesty suits you – keep it up.

MARIO. Excellent. But this 'mam'selle' business is much too formal. Between people of your sort, the mode of address shouldn't be so stilted, otherwise you'd be constantly minding your p's and q's. Come on, unbend a little – you're called Lisette, and you, my good fellow – what's your name?

DORANTE. Bourguignon, sir, at your service.

SILVIA. Very well – Bourguignon it is.

DORANTE. Lisette, then – and no less at your service.

MARIO. Good heavens, man, you don't say 'at your service' to a servant. Where are your manners?

ORGON. Ha! Ha! Ha!

SILVIA (*aside to* MARIO). You're making fun of me, dear brother.

DORANTE. Sir, as far as any kind of familiarity is concerned, I shall await the young lady's command.

SILVIA. Call me whatever you like, then, Bourguignon – the ice is clearly broken now, since it amuses these gentlemen.

DORANTE. Thank you, my dear Lisette – as you see, I am responding immediately to the honour you do me.

ORGON. Bravo, my children – once you start falling for each other, you'll soon dispense with the formalities.

MARIO. Now, wait just a moment. As for their falling for each other, that's a very different matter. Perhaps you're not aware of it, but I have my own heart set on the lovely Lisette. True enough, she's playing hard to get, but the last thing I need is this Bourguignon fellow poaching on my preserves.

SILVIA. Well, if that's the tone you're going to adopt, I *want* Bourguignon to fall in love with me!

DORANTE. Dearest Lisette, you do yourself a wrong to say 'want'. You don't need to command to have my devoted service.

MARIO. Oh, come on, Bourguignon – you must have stolen that compliment from somewhere.

DORANTE. That's true, sir – I found it in her eyes.

MARIO. Oh, be quiet, that's even worse. I forbid you to have so much wit.

SILVIA. It's not costing you anything. If he finds it in my eyes, all he has to do is take it.

ORGON. You're losing your case, my boy. Let's go now, and tell my daughter that Dorante will be here shortly. Lisette, show this fellow his master's apartment. Goodbye, Bourguignon.

DORANTE. Sir, you do me too much honour.

Exeunt ORGON *and* MARIO.

SILVIA (*aside*). They're having a good laugh at me. No matter, we'll use everything to our advantage. This young man is no fool, and I don't feel sorry for the maid who gets him. He's obviously going to flirt with me. Well, let him, as long as it's instructive.

DORANTE (*aside*). This is an amazing girl! There isn't a woman in the world who wouldn't be proud of such a face. I must get to know her better . . . . (*Aloud.*) Since we're now on friendly terms, and can dispense with the

formalities, tell me, my dear Lisette, is your mistress
worthy of you? She must be very brave, if she dares to
keep a maid like you.

SILVIA. That question, Bourguignon, tells me that you've
come with the intention of whispering sweet nothings to
me, as is no doubt your custom – isn't that so?

DORANTE. Indeed no, I came with no such intention, I
assure you. I may be a mere valet, but I've never had any
involvement to speak of with ladies' maids – I don't find
servants particularly attractive or clever. You, on the
other hand, are an entirely different matter. Good
heavens, you overwhelm me, to the point I feel almost
timid. I hardly dare use my customary familiarity with
you. I keep wanting to take my hat off to you, and when
I call you by your first name, it's as if I'm swearing. In
short, I have the strangest inclination to treat you with a
degree of respect that would make you laugh. Just what
kind of lady's maid are you, then, with the aura of a
princess?

SILVIA. Well, everything you say you feel on seeing me is
exactly what other valets have experienced – they all tell
the same story.

DORANTE. Indeed, and I wouldn't be at all surprised if
their masters felt the same way.

SILVIA. It's a pretty compliment, for sure, but let me tell
you again – I'm not easily flattered by people dressed in
your fashion.

DORANTE. You mean you don't like my clothes?

SILVIA. No, Bourguignon. Now, let's put love aside, and
just be good friends.

DORANTE. Is that all? Your little proposal consists of two impossible clauses.

SILVIA (*aside*). What a man to be a valet! (*Aloud.*) Nonetheless, you'll have to accept it. Someone told me once that I would only marry a gentleman, and ever since then I've sworn not to entertain anything less.

DORANTE. Now, isn't that funny? I've sworn exactly the same thing about women, as you have about men. I've vowed never to love seriously anyone but a lady of quality.

SILVIA. You mustn't be distracted from your goal, then.

DORANTE. But perhaps I'm not being distracted as much as we think. You have an air of great distinction, and it's possible to be a person of quality without knowing it.

SILVIA. Really? Well, now, I'd thank you for the kind thought, if it weren't at my mother's expense.

DORANTE. You can take your revenge on my mother, then, if you think I look the part.

SILVIA (*aside*). He would deserve it, too. (*Aloud.*) But that's not the point at issue. Let's call a halt to this banter. It's been foretold that a man of quality would be my husband, and I'm not going to be sold short.

DORANTE. Heavens, if I were such a man, I'd find your prophecy a threat – I fear I'd make it come true. I've no faith at all in astrology, but I have a great deal in your face.

SILVIA (*aside*). He won't give up. (*Aloud.*) Oh, do stop, please. What does the prophecy matter to you, if you're excluded anyway?

DORANTE. Well, it didn't say that I wouldn't love you.

SILVIA. No, but it did say you would gain nothing by it, and I'm simply confirming that.

DORANTE. You're doing the right thing, Lisette. This pride of yours suits you wonderfully well, and even though it puts me through the mill, I'm delighted to see it in you. From the moment I saw you, I hoped to find that pride – it was the one grace you seemed to lack, and I take some comfort from losing by it, since you gain so much.

SILVIA (*aside*). In truth, this young man surprises me, in spite of myself. (*Aloud.*) So tell me, who exactly are you, that speaks to me this way?

DORANTE. The son of honest folk, who weren't rich.

SILVIA. Well, I sincerely wish you were in a better situation, and I wish I could contribute to that. Fortune hasn't been kind to you.

DORANTE. Indeed, love has been even less kind. I would rather be allowed to ask for your heart than have all the riches in the world.

SILVIA (*aside*). Heavens above! He's openly courting me! (*Aloud.*) Bourguignon, I can't be angry with you for what you've just said, but please, let's change the subject. Let's get back to your master – and perhaps you can manage that without talking of love to me.

DORANTE. Perhaps you can manage without making me *feel* it.

SILVIA. Now I *will* get angry! You're trying my patience. Let's just forget about your love, all right?

DORANTE. Let's just forget about your face, then.

SILVIA (*aside*). He's got me so I can hardly think straight. (*Aloud.*) Well, Bourguignon – if you won't stop, I'm afraid I'll have to leave you. (*Aside.*) I should have done so already.

DORANTE. No, wait, Lisette. There was something else I wanted to say to you, but I can't remember what it was.

SILVIA. And there was something I wanted to say to you, too, but you've put it right out of my head.

DORANTE. Ah, I remember asking you if your mistress was worthy of you.

SILVIA. You've taken a detour to return to your theme. Goodbye.

DORANTE. No, Lisette, honestly – it's only my master I'm concerned with now.

.SILVIA. All right, then – I wanted to talk about him too, and I'm hoping you'll tell me in confidence what kind of man he is. The fact that you're in his service certainly raises him in my estimation. He must have some merit, if you're his servant.

DORANTE. Well now, perhaps you will allow me to thank you for what you've just said?

SILVIA. And will you kindly take no notice of my foolishness in saying it?

DORANTE. Again, another of these answers that make my head spin! Do as you will, I can't resist you – I'm truly unfortunate, to find myself detained by the most lovable creature on earth.

SILVIA. And I would like to know how it is that I'm happy to stand here listening to you – it really is most peculiar.

DORANTE. You're right – this is a unique situation.

SILVIA (*aside*). Despite everything he's said to me, I haven't left, I'm not leaving, I'm still here, answering him! In truth, this is getting beyond a joke. (*Aloud.*) Goodbye.

DORANTE. Let's finish what we were trying to say.

SILVIA. No, goodbye, and that's final – no more indulgence. When your master arrives, I'll try and find out about him myself, on my mistress's behalf – to see if he's worth bothering about. Meanwhile, this room you see is yours.

DORANTE. Ah, here comes my master now.

Enter ARLEQUIN.

ARLEQUIN. Ah, there you are, Bourguignon. My baggage and yourself – have you been well received?

DORANTE. We couldn't possibly have been received badly, sir.

ARLEQUIN. One of the servants outside told me to come in. He said he'd let my father-in-law, who's with my wife, know I'd arrived.

SILVIA. I presume you mean Monsieur Orgon and his daughter, sir?

ARLEQUIN. Well, yes – father-in-law and wife, as good as. I've come to get wed, and they're waiting for me to tie the knot. It's all been agreed – we've just the ceremony to go through, and that's a mere trifle.

SILVIA. It's a trifle well worth thinking about.

ARLEQUIN. Yes, but once you've thought about it, you can put it out of your mind.

SILVIA (*aside to* DORANTE). Well, Bourguignon, persons
of quality must come rather cheap in your part of the
world.

ARLEQUIN. What's that you're saying to my valet,
sweetheart?

SILVIA. Oh, nothing – I just said I was going to fetch
Monsieur Orgon.

ARLEQUIN. Why don't you call him my father-in-law,
same as I do?

SILVIA. Because he actually isn't.

DORANTE. She's right, sir – the marriage hasn't happened
yet.

ARLEQUIN. So? I'm here to make it happen.

DORANTE. Then you'd better wait till it does.

ARLEQUIN. Ye gods, who cares? Father-in-law today or
tomorrow, what difference does it make?

SILVIA. Indeed, what difference is there between being
married and not married? Yes, sir, we're obviously in the
wrong, and I'll run off now and tell your father-in-law
you've arrived.

ARLEQUIN. Oh, and tell my wife also, please. But before
you go, just tell me one thing. You're an extremely pretty
girl – you wouldn't by chance be the maid around here?

SILVIA. By chance I would, yes.

ARLEQUIN. Well, that's nice to know – I'm delighted. Do
you think I'll do well here? How do you find me, eh?

SILVIA. I find you . . . interesting.

ARLEQUIN. Good, excellent – just keep hold of that
sentiment, you never know your luck.

SILVIA. You must be a very modest person, sir, if that makes you happy. Anyway, I have to go now, since nobody seems to have told your father-in-law you're here, otherwise he'd surely have come.

ARLEQUIN. Right, go and tell him – I'm looking forward to meeting him.

SILVIA (*aside*). What a strange thing Fate is – neither of these two is in his rightful place.

She goes out.

ARLEQUIN. Well, sir, I've made a good start, haven't I. The maid fancies me already.

DORANTE. What a prize idiot you are!

ARLEQUIN. What do you mean? I was the soul of politeness.

DORANTE. You gave me your word that you'd keep your silly comments to yourself. And I specifically instructed you to be serious. God, I must have been out of my mind to trust you.

ARLEQUIN. I'll do better next time, honestly. And if serious won't do the trick, I'll be downright melancholy – I'll even turn on the waterworks.

DORANTE. I hardly know where I am any longer. This business has got me completely confused. What am I going to do?

ARLEQUIN. She's a nice-looking girl, don't you think?

DORANTE. Oh, be quiet. Monsieur Orgon's coming.

Enter ORGON.

ORGON. My dear sir – a thousand pardons for keeping you waiting, but I've only just this minute learned of your arrival.

ARLEQUIN. Oh, a thousand pardons is far too many, sir. You only need one, if you've only made one mistake. As for the rest, well, all my pardons are at your service.

ORGON. I'll try not to need them.

ARLEQUIN. You are the master, sir, and I'm your humble servant.

ORGON. Anyway, I can assure you I'm delighted to see you – I've been so looking forward to meeting you.

ARLEQUIN. I would have come straight in with Bourguignon, but after a long journey, you understand, one's a bit of a wreck, and I needed some time to make myself look more appetising, so to speak.

ORGON. Well, I must say you've succeeded admirably, sir. My daughter's getting dressed. She's been a trifle indisposed. Now, while we're waiting for her to come down, would you care for a little refreshment?

ARLEQUIN. Oh, I've never turned down a drink with anyone.

ORGON. And Bourguignon, you take care of yourself, my lad.

ARLEQUIN. He's a noted wine buff, you know – he'll have nothing but the best.

ORGON. Well, he needn't stint himself.

ACT TWO

ORGON, LISETTE.

ORGON. Well, now, Lisette, what is it you want?

LISETTE. Sir, I'd like a word with you.

ORGON. What about?

LISETTE. I need to tell you how things stand, sir, because it's important you should be clear about them, so you'll have no reason to complain against me.

ORGON. This is serious, then.

LISETTE. Yes, very serious. You consented to Mam'selle Silvia disguising herself, and at first I thought there was no harm in it, but it seems I've been mistaken.

ORGON. So, what harm has it done?

LISETTE. Sir, I'm reluctant to praise myself, but despite keeping strictly to all the rules of modesty, I have to tell you that if you don't sort this business out, your would-be son-in-law won't have a heart left to present to your daughter. The time has come for her to reveal herself, and quickly, too – if another day goes by, I won't be held responsible for what happens.

ORGON. Eh? What makes you think he won't want my daughter once he gets to know her? Have you no faith in her charms?

LISETTE. Indeed no, sir. But you have too little faith in mine, it seems. Sir, I must warn you they're beginning to take effect, and I advise you not to let them.

ORGON (*laughs*). Well, my compliments to you, Lisette –
bravo!

LISETTTE. Oh, I see – you think this is funny, sir. You're
laughing at me. Well, I'm sorry, but you won't be
laughing for long.

ORGON. Don't worry about it, Lisette – just go about your
business.

LISETTE. Sir, I'll say it again – Dorante's affections are
moving fast. Seriously, he's very fond of me just now, by
this evening he'll be in love with me, and tomorrow he'll
adore me. You can say what you like – I don't deserve it,
it's in extremely bad taste – but that won't stop it
happening. Just wait and see, sir, I'm going to be adored
tomorrow, I guarantee it.

ORGON. Well, so what? If he loves you that much, then let
him marry you.

LISETTE. What? You wouldn't prevent it?

ORGON. My word of honour, Lisette – no, if you bring
him to that point.

LISETTE. Sir, be careful – so far I haven't even tried to
exercise my charms on him. I've simply let them work by
themselves. I've been absolutely scrupulous about that.
But if I get started, I'll overwhelm him for sure – he
won't stand a chance.

ORGON. Overwhelm him, then, set him on fire, take him
by storm – in a word, marry him. I'll permit it, if you
can do it.

LISETTE. Well, if that's the position, my fortune's as good
as made.

ORGON. But tell me, Lisette – has my daughter said anything to you about her fiancé? What does she think of him?

LISETTE. We've scarcely found a moment to speak, sir – her fiancé never leaves my side. But judging by appearances, I don't think she's pleased – she seems sad, and preoccupied, and I fully expect her to tell me to send him packing.

ORGON. Well, I forbid you to do that. I'm avoiding discussing it with her, but I have my reasons for prolonging this disguise. I want her to have plenty of time to consider her future husband. But what about the valet – how is he conducting himself? He isn't by chance falling in love with my daughter, is he?

LISETTE. Oh, he's a strange character, sir. I've noticed that he acts quite the gentleman with her, since he's really rather handsome – and he keeps looking at her and sighing.

ORGON. And does that annoy her?

LISETTE. Actually, she blushes.

ORGON. No, you're mistaken – having a valet sigh for her surely wouldn't embarrass her.

LISETTE. Sir, she blushes.

ORGON. Well, of course, from sheer indignation.

LISETTE. If you say so, sir.

ORGON. Anyway, when you next see her, tell her you suspect this valet of trying to turn her against his master. Don't worry if she gets angry – I'll attend to that. Ah, now here comes Dorante – obviously looking for you.

Enter ARLEQUIN.

ARLEQUIN. Ah, I've found you at last, you wonderful creature! I've been asking for you all over the place. Your humble servant, dear father-in-law, or nearly so.

ORGON. Good day, sir, and goodbye, my children. I shall leave you alone together – it's as well you should grow to love each other a little before marriage.

ARLEQUIN. Indeed, sir, I'd be happy to do both jobs – love her and marry her as well.

ORGON. Don't be impatient, though. Goodbye.

Exit ORGON.

ARLEQUIN. Madame, he tells me not to be impatient – that's easy enough for him to say, at his age.

LISETTE. I'm not convinced you find waiting such torment, sir. You're only pretending to be impatient out of gallantry. After all, you've only just arrived here, your love can't be that strong, new-born as it is.

ARLEQUIN. No, you're mistaken, you miraculous being. Love such as you inspire doesn't stay long in the cradle. Your very first glance gave birth to my love, your second gave him strength, and your third made a fine strapping lad of him. Now we must marry him off as soon as possible. You're his mother, after all, so you must take good care of him.

LISETTE. What, do you think he's been maltreated, or neglected?

ARLEQUIN. Well, until he's properly provided for, at least give him your beautiful white hand, just to play with a little.

LISETTE. There you are, then, you demanding little creature, since it's the only way I'll get any peace.

ARLEQUIN (*kissing her hand*). Ah, sweet plaything of my heart! This makes me as happy as the most delicious wine – what a pity it's only a thimbleful!

LISETTE. Now, stop, you're being too greedy.

ARLEQUIN. All I want is a little nourishment to keep me alive.

LISETTE. Why can't you be more reasonable?

ARLEQUIN. Reasonable? Alas, I've lost my reason – your beautiful eyes are the villains who've stolen it from me.

LISETTE. Is it really possible that you love me so much? I can't make myself believe it.

ARLEQUIN. I don't care about what's possible – all I know is that I love you like a man possessed. Just look in your mirror, and you'll see the reason why.

LISETTE. Sir, my mirror will only serve to make me more incredulous.

ARLEQUIN. Oh, my adorable little darling! Such humility could only ever be hypocrisy.

LISETTE. Someone's coming – it's your valet.

Enter DORANTE.

DORANTE. Sir, may I have a word with you?

ARLEQUIN. No. And damn the whole villainous crew of valets who can't leave a person in peace.

LISETTE. You'd better see what he wants, sir.

DORANTE. Just one word, if you please.

ARLEQUIN. Madame, if he says two words, the third will be his dismissal. Right, let's hear it.

DORANTE (*to* ARLEQUIN, *sotto voce*). Why, you impudent scoundrel!

ARLEQUIN (*to* DORANTE, *sotto voce*). Sir, these are insults, not words . . . (*To* LISETTE.) If you'll excuse me, my queen?

LISETTE. Go ahead.

DORANTE. Now stop all this carry-on, but don't give yourself away. You've got to appear serious and thoughtful – unhappy, even, do you understand?

ARLEQUIN. Yes, of course, my friend. Don't worry about it – now leave us alone, please.

Exit DORANTE.

ARLEQUIN (*to* LISETTE). Ah, but for him, I would have said the most wonderful things to you, and now I'll only be able to find ordinary ones – apart from my love, which is extraordinary. But speaking of my love, when will yours keep mine company?

LISETTE. We can only hope that it'll happen.

ARLEQUIN. And do you think that it'll happen soon?

LISETTE. That's the burning question. Actually, you're making me feel quite uncomfortable.

ARLEQUIN. Well, what do you expect? *I'm* burning, so I'm shouting 'Fire!'

LISETTE. If I were permitted to reveal my feelings so quickly . . .

ARLEQUIN. My feeling is that you can speak freely.

LISETTE. No, the modesty of my sex won't allow it.

ARLEQUIN. That's not modesty these days, then – that allows all sorts of things.

LISETTE. What is it you want from me?

ARLEQUIN. Tell me you love me just a tiny bit. Look, I love you, so be my echo. Repeat after me, princess.

LISETTE. Oh, the man's insatiable! Very well, sir – I love you.

ARLEQUIN. Oh, madame, I'm dying. I'm so overcome with joy, I fear I'll run mad. You love me – that's wonderful!

LISETTE. For my part, I ought to be amazed at how quickly you've declared your devotion. Perhaps you'll love me less when we're better acquainted.

ARLEQUIN. Ah, madame, when we reach that point, I stand to lose a great deal – I won't be worth much.

LISETTE. You credit me with more quality than I possess.

ARLEQUIN. And you, madame, have no idea of mine. I really ought to be speaking to you on my knees.

LISETTE. Just remember that we're not the masters of our fate.

ARLEQUIN. No, fathers and mothers do as they see fit.

LISETTE. Personally speaking, my heart would have chosen you whatever your station in life.

ARLEQUIN. It'll have an excellent chance to choose me again, then.

LISETTE. May I flatter myself that you feel the same way about me?

ARLEQUIN. Madame, if you had been the meanest serving-wench, and I'd seen you going down to the cellar with a candle in your hand, you'd still have been my princess.

LISETTE. Let's hope such noble sentiments are long-lasting!

ARLEQUIN. To strengthen them on both sides, let's swear to love each other always, regardless of any mistaken ideas you may have about me.

LISETTE. I have more to gain from such a vow than you, and I swear it with all my heart.

ARLEQUIN (*kneels*). I'm dazzled by your kindness, and I kneel before it.

LISETTE. No, stop – I can't allow you to stay in that position, it would be ridiculous of me. Stand up, sir. Oh, there's someone coming!

Enter SILVIA.

LISETTE. What is it you want, Lisette?

SILVIA. I need to speak with you, madame.

ARLEQUIN. Oh, for goodness' sake! Look, my dear, come back in a quarter of an hour. Go on – maids in my neck of the woods don't come in unless they're called.

SILVIA. Sir, I really need to speak to madame.

ARLEQUIN. Would you listen to the obstinate hussy? Send her away, queen of my heart. Now clear off, my girl – we've been ordered to love each other before we get married, and you're keeping us from our work.

LISETTE. Can't you come back a bit later, Lisette?

SILVIA. But, madame . . .

ARLEQUIN. But? This 'but' just makes my blood boil.

SILVIA (*aside*). Oh, the vile wretch! (*Aloud.*) Madame, I assure you, it really is important.

LISETTE. Oh, all right. Sir, if you'll allow me to deal with this . . .

ARLEQUIN. Well, since the devil demands, and her too . . . Patience, patience . . . I'll go for a stroll until she's done. These servants of ours really are idiots!

He goes out.

SILVIA. Lisette, I'm amazed that you didn't send him out straight away, and that you've forced me to endure the downright rudeness of that nasty creature.

LISETTE. Good heavens, madame, I can't play two parts at the same time. I've got to be either mistress or servant – give orders or take them.

SILVIA. Well, all right, but since he's no longer here, listen to me as your mistress. I'm sure you can see that that man doesn't suit me at all.

LISETTE. But you haven't had the time to study him closely.

SILVIA. Study? Has your studying driven you mad? Do you need a second look at him to see just how unsuitable he is? In short, I want nothing to do with him. However, it seems my father doesn't approve of my revulsion, since he's avoiding me, and not saying a word. In which case, it's up to you to extricate me from this business, by tactfully letting this young man know you have no desire to marry him.

LISETTE. I can't do that, madame.

SILVIA. You can't do that! What's stopping you?

LISETTE. Monsieur Orgon has forbidden me.

SILVIA. He's forbidden you? My father? No, I don't believe it, that's not like him at all.

LISETTE. Strictly forbidden.

SILVIA. Very well, then, I'm ordering you to inform him of my distaste for this man, and to assure him that nothing will overcome it. I can't imagine he'll want to pursue the matter any further after that.

LISETTE. But, madame, why do you dislike him so much – what is it you find so repulsive about your future husband?

SILVIA. I just don't like him, I tell you, and I don't like your lack of support either.

LISETTE. At least give yourself time to see what he's like, that's all you're being asked.

SILVIA. I hate him quite enough already, I don't need time to hate him even more.

LISETTE. That valet of his, with his self-important airs – he wouldn't by any chance have turned you against his master?

SILVIA. Oh, don't be silly! His valet has absolutely nothing to do with it.

LISETTE. Well, I don't trust him: he's too clever by half.

SILVIA. And that's enough of your opinions, I can do without them. Anyway, I take good care not to let the valet say much to me, and the few things he *has* said, have never been less than entirely sensible.

LISETTE. Well, I get the feeling he's the kind of man who'll tell you all sorts of nonsense, just to show off his dazzling wit.

SILVIA. Look, my disguise compels me to listen to compliments, if that's what you mean. But what have you got against him? What makes you so determined to blame this young man for feelings of revulsion he's got nothing to do with? I mean, really – you're forcing me to defend him now, but there's no question of trying to cause trouble for him with his master, or making him out to be a rogue, just so you can present me as a fool for listening to his stories.

LISETTE. Well, madame, if you're going to take that tone in his defence, losing your temper into the bargain, I'll say no more.

SILVIA. Take that tone in his defence? And what tone are you taking yourself? What exactly do you mean by that remark? What's going on in your mind?

LISETTE. I'm just saying, madame, that I've never seen you like this before, and I don't know why you're being so sharp with me. All right, if this valet really hasn't said anything, that's fine, you don't need to fly into a rage to defend him. I believe you, and that's that. I'm not going to contradict the good opinion you have of him.

SILVIA. What a nasty creature! Honestly, the way she twists things! It makes me so angry, I feel I could cry . . .

LISETTE. What on earth for, madame? Twist what things? What have I said?

SILVIA. All those sly hints, yes – I'm defending him against you! I have a good opinion of him! That just shows how little respect you have for me. A good opinion? Heavens above! Good opinion! What am I supposed to say to that? What do you mean by that, who do you think you're talking to? Is nobody safe from this sort of attack? What have we come to?

LISETTE. Madame, I have no idea, but it'll be a long time before I get over the shock you've given me.

SILVIA. Honestly, the way she puts things is driving me crazy. Go away, I can't stand you any longer. Leave me alone, I'll find some other means . . .

Exit LISETTE.

I'm still trembling from what I've just heard her say. The impertinent way these servants look on us behind our backs! It's so degrading! I don't know how I'll recover from this, and I daren't even think of the expressions she used, I'm still frightened by them. I mean, we're talking about a valet! Really, what an absurd idea! And that insolent creature has tainted my imagination with it – I must put it out of my mind. Here's Bourguignon now – the object of my . . . the person I'm losing my temper over. Well, it's not his fault, poor boy, I'm not going to take it out on him.

Enter DORANTE.

DORANTE. Lisette, no matter how distant you feel from me, I am compelled to speak to you. I think you have given me cause for complaint.

SILVIA. Oh, dearest Bourguignon, please don't call me Lisette – we mustn't be so familiar with each other.

DORANTE. If that's what you want, Lisette.

SILVIA. But you're still doing it.

DORANTE. And so are you – you called me 'dearest' just now.

SILVIA. That was a slip of the tongue.

DORANTE. Well, let's just speak as we've been doing – it's not worth bothering about, given how short a time we have together.

SILVIA. What, is your master leaving? That won't be any great loss.

DORANTE. And no great loss if I go either, I daresay? Just to complete your thought.

SILVIA. I could complete it myself, if I wished, but no, I wasn't thinking about you.

DORANTE. Whereas I think of nothing *but* you.

SILVIA. Look, Bourguignon, once and for all – whether you stay or go, or come back, shouldn't really interest me, and as a matter of fact it doesn't. I wish you neither well nor ill – I neither hate you nor love you, nor will I ever love you unless I take leave of my senses entirely. That's the state of my feelings at present, my reason won't permit me to feel any other way, and I shouldn't even have to tell you this.

DORANTE. You have no idea how unhappy I am – you may have taken away my peace of mind forever.

SILVIA (*aside*). What a bizarre idea he's got hold of! He's really upsetting me. (*Aloud.*) Look, pull yourself together. You're speaking to me, and I'm replying. That's quite a lot, too much, even, believe me. If you knew your place, you'd be quite content with that – you'd regard me as the very soul of kindness, a kindness, incidentally, which I would condemn in anyone else. But I'm not reproaching myself for that – deep down, my heart assures me that what I am doing is only to be praised. I'm speaking to you out of simple generosity. This can't last, however – generous impulses like that are spur-of-the-moment things, and I'm not the sort of person who can always be sure of the innocence of her intentions. In a word, it just doesn't make any sense. So let's put an end to this, Bourguignon, please. What does it all mean? We're just making fools of ourselves, let's say no more on the subject.

DORANTE. Oh, my dearest Lisette, I'm in such pain!

LISETTE. Let's get back to what you started to say. You said you had some cause for complaint about me when you came into the room – what was that about?

DORANTE. Nothing, nothing at all – I simply wanted to see you, and I think I just used that as an excuse.

SILVIA (aside). What can I say to that? If I get angry, it won't make the slightest difference.

DORANTE. As she was going out, your mistress seemed to be accusing me of having spoken ill of my master.

SILVIA. She's imagining things. If she mentions it again, deny it strongly. I'll take care of the rest.

DORANTE. That's not what's worrying me.

SILVIA. Well, if that's all you have to say, I think we're finished here.

DORANTE. At least leave me the pleasure of seeing you.

SILVIA. A fine motive he gives me for staying! I'm supposed to indulge Bourguignon's passion. One of these days I'll look back and laugh at all this.

DORANTE. You're poking fun at me, but you're right – I don't know what I'm saying, or what I'm asking for. Goodbye.

SILVIA. Goodbye – you're doing the right thing . . . On the subject of goodbyes, though, there's one more thing I'd like to know. You said you were leaving – were you serious?

DORANTE. For my part, I've either got to leave, or go mad.

SILVIA. That's not the kind of answer I called you back for.

DORANTE. And I've made only one mistake – which was not to leave the moment I saw you.

SILVIA (*aside*). I need to forget I'm listening to him, every second.

DORANTE. If only you knew, dearest Lisette, the state I find myself in.

SILVIA. It's not as strange as mine, I can assure you.

DORANTE. What can you reproach me with? I'm not trying to make you fall in love with me.

SILVIA (*aside*). I wouldn't be too sure of that.

DORANTE. And what could I hope to achieve by trying to make you love me? Alas, even if I did win your heart . . .

SILVIA. Which God forbid! If you were to win it, you wouldn't know it, and I'd take great pains to ensure that I didn't know it either. Honestly, the very idea!

DORANTE. So, is it true then that you neither hate me nor love me, and never will love me?

SILVIA. Without hesitation – yes.

DORANTE. Without hesitation? What's so awful about me, then?

SILVIA. Nothing – that isn't what counts against you.

DORANTE. Very well, dearest Lisette – tell me a hundred times that you won't ever love me.

SILVIA. I've told you that enough, just try and believe me.

DORANTE. I've got to believe you. Make me despair of this dangerous passion – that's the only way to save me from its frightening consequences. You don't hate me, you don't love me, you'll never love me – crush my heart with that certainty! I'm acting in good faith, help me against myself, I need your help, I'm begging you on my knees!

He falls to his knees. At this point, enter ORGON *and* MARIO, *without speaking.*

SILVIA. Oh, heavens, look at this! That's all this little adventure of mine was needing. I feel so wretched – it's my own indulgence that's brought him to this position. Get up, Bourguignon, please, I beg you – somebody could come in. I'll say anything you like, what do you want me to say? I honestly don't hate you, please stand up – I would love you if I could, I don't find you at all unattractive – that ought to be enough, surely?

DORANTE. Dearest Lisette, what if I weren't who I am? Supposing I were rich, of noble rank, and loved you as much as I do now – would your heart feel no revulsion towards me?

SILVIA. None whatever, I assure you.

DORANTE. You wouldn't hate me? You'd be prepared to suffer me?

SILVIA. Willingly, but please stand up.

DORANTE. You seem to mean what you say, and if that's so, I'm surely losing my mind.

SILVIA. I'm saying what you want, and you're not standing up yet.

ORGON. It's a great pity to interrupt you, my dears, when everything's going so wonderfully well – but be of good heart!

SILVIA. Sir, I'm afraid I couldn't stop this young man falling to his knees. I'm in no position to command his respect, as far as I know.

ORGON. You two are perfectly well suited to each other, but I'd like a word with you, Lisette, and you can continue your conversation after we've gone. Would you excuse us, Bourguignon?

DORANTE. I shall withdraw, sir.

ORGON. Off you go, then, and try to speak of your master with a little more deference than you've been showing.

DORANTE. Me, sir?

ORGON. Yes, you, monsieur Bourguignon. From what I hear, you're not exactly a shining example in that regard.

DORANTE. I don't know what you mean, sir.

ORGON. Anyway, goodbye – you can explain yourself some other time.

Exit DORANTE.

ORGON. Well, Silvia, you're not looking at us – you seem rather embarrassed.

SILVIA. Me, father? What cause would I have to be embarrassed? I'm just my usual self, thank heavens. I'm sorry to say it, but you're imagining things.

MARIO. No, there's something going on, dear sister, there definitely is.

SILVIA. Something going on in your head, dear brother, but as far as mine is concerned, there's nothing but astonishment at what you're saying.

ORGON. So this young man who's just gone out – is he the one who has inspired you with such antipathy towards his master?

SILVIA. Who? Dorante's valet?

ORGON. Yes, the gallant monsieur Bourguignon.

SILVIA. Gallant? I don't recognise the description, but he never says anything to me about his master.

ORGON. Nevertheless, the word is that he has somehow discredited his master with you, and that's what I'm anxious to speak to you about.

SILVIA. Well, you're wasting your time, father. Nobody in the world, apart from his master himself, is responsible for the natural aversion I feel towards him.

MARIO. Why, that's nonsense, dear sister – your aversion to him is far too strong to be natural. Someone must have prompted you.

SILVIA (*animatedly*). What are you insinuating? What are all these mysterious hints? Who's this person who's supposed to have prompted me? Come on, out with it!

MARIO. Really, sister, there's no need to fly off the handle!

SILVIA. Frankly, I'm sick and tired of playing this part, and I'd have taken off my disguise long ago if I wasn't afraid of upsetting my father.

ORGON. You'll do no such thing, my dear – that's just what I came to tell you. Since I indulged you by permitting this disguise, you'll kindly indulge me by suspending your judgment of Dorante, until you see whether this aversion you've acquired towards him is justified.

SILVIA. You're not even listening to me, father. There's no other person involved, I'm telling you.

MARIO. What, this smooth-tongued creature who's just gone out, hasn't put you off his master, even just a little?

SILVIA (*heatedly*). What a nasty thing to say! Put me off him? Put me off? Why do I have to suffer these insults? It's very strange, and quite uncalled for – nothing but veiled hints and insinuations, all couched in the most peculiar language: I 'seem rather embarrassed', 'there's something going on' – next it's this 'gallant' Bourguignon, so-called, who has 'put me off' his master. Well, you can say whatever you like, but I don't understand any of it.

MARIO. Not at all – you're the one who's strange. Who are you blaming for this? What's making you so touchy? What do you suspect us of?

SILVIA. Go on, dear brother. What, is it just my bad luck that everything you say today appals me? What suspicions would you like me to have? Are you seeing things now?

ORGON. Well, it's true – you're so worked up I hardly recognise you. I don't doubt it was these emotional

outbursts that made Lisette speak to us the way she did.
It seems she suggested that this valet might not have
spoken too favourably of his master, and, 'Madame,' she
told us, 'sprang to his defence so fiercely that I'm still
quite astonished.' We took issue with her over the word
'astonished', but people of her sort don't always
understand the consequences a word might have.

SILVIA. Why, the brazen hussy! Could anyone be more
hateful than that creature? I lost my temper a little, that's
all, out of a sense of justice on that young man's behalf.

MARIO. I don't see any harm in that.

SILVIA. What could be more straightforward? Just because
I'm fair-minded, because I don't like seeing people hurt,
because I want to save a servant from getting into trouble
with his master, she says I'm having a fit or something,
and that she's astonished! And next minute, the spiteful
creature starts telling stories. So someone has to get
angry with her, someone has to tell her to shut up,
someone has to take my side – all because of the
consequences of what she's said? I need someone to
defend me, I need to be justified, do I? People can see
something wrong in what I'm doing? Well, what have I
actually done? What am I being accused of? Tell me,
please do. Is this serious? Or are you just making a fool of
me? I find this very upsetting.

ORGON. Then calm down, my dear.

SILVIA. Calm down? That's hardly in order, with this
'astonishment' and 'consequences'! Explanations, that's
what we need – yes, what does it mean? People are
accusing this valet, and they're quite wrong. You've made
a mistake, all of you, and Lisette is a fool – he's innocent

and that's the end of it. I don't want to hear another word about it. Frankly, I'm very angry.

ORGON. You're keeping your feelings in check, my dear – you'd obviously like to rage at me as well. However, we'll sort everything out – it's only the valet who's under suspicion here, and all Dorante has to do is dismiss him.

SILVIA. Oh, this wretched disguise! Lisette had better not come near me, I hate her more than I do Dorante.

ORGON. You don't need to see her unless you want to, but you ought to be pleased that this young man's leaving, since he's in love with you, and that must be a nuisance.

SILVIA. I can't very well complain about that – he takes me for a servant, and addresses me accordingly. But he doesn't say just whatever he likes, I make sure of that.

MARIO. I don't think you're as much in control of the situation as you claim.

ORGON. Didn't we just see him go down on his knees before you, against your wishes? Weren't you obliged to tell him you didn't dislike him, to make him get up?

SILVIA (*aside*). I feel as if I'm choking!

MARIO. And what's more, when he asked you if you *would* love him, you had to say, 'Willingly!', with real feeling, otherwise he'd still be there on his knees!

SILVIA. What an apt footnote, dear brother. But I didn't appreciate the scene in the first place, and I like having it replayed even less. To be serious, just when is this comedy you're enjoying at my expense going to end?

ORGON. All I'm asking of you, my dear child, is that you don't make up your mind to reject him without knowing

all the facts. Just wait a little longer – you'll thank me for
the delay, I promise you.

MARIO. You will marry Dorante, and willingly too, that I
can confidently predict. But I'd ask you to have mercy on
the valet, father.

SILVIA. Why mercy? I want him to leave.

ORGON. His master can decide. Now, let's go.

MARIO. Goodbye, dear sister, and no hard feelings, eh?

Exeunt ORGON *and* MARIO.

SILVIA. Oh, my aching heart! I don't know what it is about
this mess I've got myself into, but I find the whole
business terribly upsetting. I can't trust anybody, it seems,
and I'm at ease with nobody, not even with myself.

Enter DORANTE.

DORANTE. Ah, Lisette, I've been looking everywhere for
you.

SILVIA. Well, you needn't have bothered finding me – I've
been avoiding you.

DORANTE. No, stay, Lisette. I need to speak to you for the
last time. It's on a matter of some importance concerning
your masters.

SILVIA. Speak to them, then. Every time I see you, you
manage to upset me. Leave me alone.

DORANTE. I can say the same about you. But listen to me,
please – you're going to see a great change taking place,
as a result of what I'm about to tell you.

SILVIA. All right, then – speak, I'm listening, since it's
obviously decreed somewhere that my indulgence
towards you shall know no bounds.

DORANTE. Will you promise to keep it secret?

SILVIA. I've never betrayed anybody.

DORANTE. I'm only sharing this secret with you, because of the high esteem I hold you in.

SILVIA. I believe it. But I wish you would esteem me without telling me – it sounds like a pretext for something.

DORANTE. No, you're mistaken, Lisette. You've promised to keep my secret, so let's get to the point. You've seen the depths of my feelings, I couldn't stop myself falling in love with you.

SILVIA. Here we go again. Well, I'll stop myself listening to you. Goodbye.

DORANTE. No, stay – this isn't Bourguignon speaking to you.

SILVIA. So who are you, then?

DORANTE. Oh, Lisette! Now you're going to understand the pain I've had to endure in my heart.

SILVIA. It's not your heart I'm talking to, it's you.

DORANTE. There's no one coming, is there?

SILVIA. No.

DORANTE. Things have reached such a state that I'm forced to tell you – I'm too honourable a man not to call a halt to them.

SILVIA. Very well.

DORANTE. Lisette, you really should know that the man who is with your mistress isn't who people think he is.

SILVIA (*brusquely*). Who is he, then?

DORANTE. A valet.

SILVIA. And?

DORANTE. And I am Dorante.

SILVIA (*aside*). Ah! I see clearly into my heart now.

DORANTE. I wanted to use this disguise to discover a little
bit about your mistress, before marrying her. My father
gave me his permission when I was leaving, and the
outcome has been like a bad dream. I hate the mistress
I was supposed to marry, and I've fallen in love with the
servant who was meant to see me only as a new master.
What am I going to do now? I blush for her to say it, but
your mistress has so little taste that she's fallen for my
valet to the point where she'll marry him if she's
permitted to. Tell me, what should I do?

SILVIA (*aside*). I won't tell him who I am. (*Aloud.*) Well, your
situation is certainly a new one on me. But, sir, I must
first apologise for any inappropriate remarks I might have
made in our conversations.

DORANTE (*brusquely*). Be quiet, Lisette! Your apologies
upset me – they only serve to remind me of the distance
that separates us, and make this even more painful.

SILVIA. Are your feelings towards me really serious, then?
Do you love me so much?

DORANTE. Enough to renounce any other engagement,
since I'm not allowed to unite my destiny with yours. And
in this situation, the only pleasure I could taste was to
believe that at least you didn't hate me.

SILVIA. A heart that has chosen me, in my lowly position, is assuredly deserving of acceptance, and I would willingly repay it with my own, if I weren't afraid of committing it to an engagement which might be to its detriment.

DORANTE. Haven't you charms enough, dear Lisette? Must you also speak to me with such nobility of spirit?

SILVIA. There's someone coming. Don't be too worried about your valet – we needn't rush things. We'll see each other again, and find some way of getting you out of this difficulty.

DORANTE. I'll follow your advice

He goes out.

SILVIA. Well, well. I really needed *that* one to be Dorante.

Enter MARIO.

MARIO. I've come to find you again, sister. We left you in such a state of anxiety that I'm genuinely upset. Anyway, I'll get you out of it, so listen to me.

SILVIA (*animatedly*). Really, brother? Well, I have some news for you.

MARIO. What is it?

SILVIA. He isn't Bourguignon at all – he's Dorante.

MARIO. Who are you talking about now?

SILVIA. Him, I'm telling you. I've just this minute found out. He's gone now, but he told me himself.

MARIO. Who did?

SILVIA. You're not listening to me, are you?

MARIO. Yes, I am, but I'll be damned if I understand any of it.

SILVIA. Oh, never mind – let's go and find father, he's got to know. I'll need you too, dear brother. I have a few new tricks up my sleeve, and I want you to pretend to be in love with me. You've already hinted as much by way of a joke. Above all else, though, you must keep it a secret.

MARIO. Oh, I'll keep it secret all right – since I don't know what it is.

SILVIA. Now, come on, let's not waste any time. I tell you, there's never been anything quite like this!

MARIO. Pray heaven she's not going mad.

ACT THREE

DORANTE, ARLEQUIN.

ARLEQUIN. But, sir – most highly esteemed master, please, I beg you.

DORANTE. Are you still going on?

ARLEQUIN. Have pity on me, sir, in my good fortune. Don't begrudge me my happiness, when things are going so well – don't stand in my way.

DORANTE. That's enough, you miserable wretch. I think you're making a fool of me. You deserve a good thrashing.

ARLEQUIN. Which I won't refuse, sir, if I deserve it, but once I've had it, please let me go and deserve some more. Would you like me to fetch your stick?

DORANTE. Villain!

ARLEQUIN. Villain I may be, but that shouldn't stop me making my fortune.

DORANTE. Scoundrel! What's he up to now?

ARLEQUIN. Scoundrel's fine too, it suits me nicely. A villain isn't dishonoured being called a scoundrel, but a scoundrel can still make a good marriage.

DORANTE. What? You insolent creature! You want me to deceive a respectable gentleman? You think I'd allow you to marry his daughter under my name? Listen, if you ever mention that piece of effrontery to me again, I'll send you packing on the spot, just as soon as I've told Monsieur Orgon who you really are – do you understand me?

ARLEQUIN. Look, sir, let's make a deal: this young lady adores me, she practically worships me. If I tell her I'm just a valet, and despite that, the tender-hearted creature still fancies a spot of wedlock with me, wouldn't you allow the violins to play?

DORANTE. As soon as they know who you really are, it's no longer my concern.

ARLEQUIN. Fine! I'm going right now to inform this generous young lady of my true station in life. I trust the trivial matter of a servant's livery won't cause us to fall out, and that her love will entitle me to a seat at the table, despite a cruel fate which left me standing by the sideboard.

He goes out.

DORANTE. Everything that's going on here, everything that's happened to me, simply passes belief . . . But I would like to see Lisette again, since she promised to get me out of this fix, to find out how she's fared with her mistress. Perhaps I can catch her on her own.

Enter MARIO.

MARIO. Wait, Bourguignon – I'd like a word with you.

DORANTE. How can I be of service to you, sir?

MARIO. You've been flirting with Lisette, I believe?

DORANTE. She's so attractive, indeed it would be hard not to, sir.

MARIO. And how does she receive your advances?

DORANTE. Sir, she makes fun of them.

MARIO. Hm, you're a clever man – you're not trying to trick me?

DORANTE. No, but what does it matter to you anyway? Supposing Lisette *had* opened her heart to me . . .

MARIO. Opened her heart! Where do you get these expressions from? That's rather high-flown for a fellow of your station.

DORANTE. Sir, I don't know any other way to talk.

MARIO. It looks as if you've been trying to seduce Lisette with little niceties of that sort – imitating a man of quality.

DORANTE. I can assure you, sir, I'm imitating nobody. But obviously you're not here just in order to mock me – you must have something else to say. We were speaking about Lisette, about my liking for her, and the interest you're taking in it.

MARIO. Ye gods! Do I detect a hint of jealousy already? You need to moderate your tone a little. Anyway, you were saying about Lisette – supposing she had opened her heart to you . . . Well, then what?

DORANTE. And exactly why should you need to know, sir?

MARIO. Ah, well – here's why. In point of fact, despite the jokey manner I adopted earlier, I should be extremely annoyed if she were to love you. So, without further debate, I forbid you to make any more advances to her. It's not because I have the slightest fear that she might fall in love with you – I think she's much too refined for that. No, I simply find it rather disagreeable to have Bourguignon as a rival.

DORANTE. Indeed, I can well believe it, for Bourguignon – however much Bourguignon he may be – isn't happy to have you as a rival either.

MARIO. Well, he'll have to get used to it.

DORANTE. I dare say he will have to. But tell me, sir – do you love her very much?

MARIO. Enough to form a serious attachment with her, as soon as I've taken certain steps. Am I making myself understood?

DORANTE. Yes, I think I know what you mean. I take it that you're sure she loves you?

MARIO. Well, what do you think? Am I not worthy of her love?

DORANTE. You don't really expect to be praised by your rivals, do you?

MARIO. That's a clever answer, and I forgive you for it. But I'm somewhat mortified that I can't say whether or not she loves me. And I'm telling you this, not by way of explanation, as you can well believe, but simply because one must tell the truth.

DORANTE. You astonish me, sir. So, Lisette knows nothing of your intentions?

MARIO. Lisette knows all the good I wish her, and seems unaffected by it, but I hope that reason will win me her heart. Anyway, no more argument – you can leave me now. Lisette's coolness towards me, despite everything I have to offer her, will have to be your only consolation for the sacrifice you'll be making. Your servant's livery isn't enough to tip the balance in your favour, and you're frankly in no position to do battle with me.

Enter SILVIA.

MARIO. Ah, Lisette – you're here.

SILVIA. Yes, sir – what is it? You seem a little upset.

MARIO. It's nothing. I was just having a word with
Bourguignon.

SILVIA. He looks sad. Have you been reprimanding him?

DORANTE. The young master was telling me that he loves
you, Lisette.

SILVIA. Well, I can't help that.

DORANTE. And he forbids me to love you.

SILVIA. Really? Does he also forbid me to seem worthy of
your love?

MARIO. I can't stop him loving you, Lisette, but I don't
want him to tell you.

SILVIA. He's stopped telling me. He's only repeating it.

MARIO. Well, at least he's not going to repeat it in my
presence. Leave us, Bourguignon.

DORANTE. I'm waiting for her to order me.

MARIO. Again?

SILVIA. He says he's waiting, have a little patience.

DORANTE. Do you feel any affection for the young
master?

SILVIA. Love, do you mean? Oh, I don't think it'll be
necessary to forbid me that.

DORANTE. Aren't you deceiving me?

MARIO. Well, honestly – this is some part I'm playing here!
Why doesn't he just leave? Who am I talking to?

DORANTE. To Bourguignon, that's all.

MARIO. Right, then let him clear off!

DORANTE (*aside*). I'm in agony!

SILVIA. Do as he says, he's getting angry.

DORANTE (*to* SILVIA). Maybe that suits you just fine.

MARIO. Come on, that's enough.

DORANTE. You didn't mention *that* love to me, Lisette.

He goes out.

Enter ORGON.

SILVIA. Now, you must admit, it would be extremely ungrateful of me *not* to love that man.

MARIO (*laughing*). Ha, ha, ha!

ORGON. What are you laughing at, Mario?

MARIO. At Dorante. He's gone out absolutely furious because I made him leave Lisette.

SILVIA. But what did he say to you in the little private chat you've just had with him?

MARIO. I've never seen a man more confused, or in a worse temper.

ORGON. Well, I'm not sorry he's been hoist with his own petard. And anyway, looking on the bright side, nothing could have been more flattering or obliging to him than what you've done up to now, my child. However, that's enough, I think.

MARIO. But just how far has this gone, sister dear?

SILVIA. Alas, dear brother, I must confess I have some reason to be happy.

MARIO. 'Alas, dear brother', she says. Can't you hear a certain sweet contentment behind those words?

ORGON. What, do you actually hope he's going to offer you his hand while you're still in disguise?

SILVIA. Oh yes, my dear father, I do hope so!

MARIO. So it's 'my dear father' now – what a saucy creature you are. You've stopped scolding us, and now you're all sweetness and light.

SILVIA. You don't let me get away with anything, do you.

MARIO. Ha, ha, I'm having my revenge. You took me to task about my expressions a short while ago, and now it's my turn to have some fun at your expense. Your delight is every bit as entertaining as your disquiet.

ORGON. Well, I won't give you any cause for complaint, my dear child – I'll go along with whatever you wish.

SILVIA. Oh, sir, if you only knew how much I'll be indebted to you. Dorante and I are truly destined for one another. He must marry me. If you only knew how grateful I'll be to him for what he's done for me today, how I will always remember the tender love he has shown me; if you only knew how delightful all this will make our blessed union – he'll never be able to recall this affair of ours without loving me, and I'll never think of it without loving him. You have sealed our happiness for life, by allowing me to do this – it's a truly unique marriage, a story to melt the heart in the very telling – it's the most extraordinary stroke of luck, the happiest, the most . . .

MARIO. Ha, ha, ha, what a chatterbox your heart is, dear sister – and so eloquent!

ORGON. I must admit it's an enchanting picture you paint, provided you can bring it about.

SILVIA. It's as good as done. Dorante is conquered, and I await my prisoner.

MARIO. The chains that bind him will be more gilded than he imagines, but I think he's suffering now and I do feel sorry for him.

SILVIA. Well, the pain it's costing him to make up his mind only makes him more worthy in my eyes. He believes that he'll upset his father by marrying me – he thinks he's betraying his birth and fortune, and these are very serious considerations. I would be delighted to triumph over them, but I need to seize victory, and not have him simply present it to me. I want to see a battle between love and reason.

MARIO. And reason must perish, of course.

ORGON. That is, you want him to feel the full extent of the folly he'll think he's committing. What insatiable vanity!

MARIO. Indeed, woman and vanity go hand in hand.

Enter LISETTE.

ORGON. Sshh! Here comes Lisette. Let's see what she wants.

LISETTE. Sir, you said a little while ago that you were leaving Dorante to me, that he was now at my disposal. I've taken you at your word, and worked on him for myself, and as you'll see I've done a good job – he's now thoroughly well conditioned. So what would you like me to do next? Is my mistress going to hand him over to me?

ORGON. What do you say, my child? Do you wish to lay claim to him?

SILVIA. No, Lisette, I'll give him to you. I'm surrendering all my rights to you, I don't want any piece of a heart which, to use your expression, I myself haven't 'conditioned'.

LISETTE. What? You don't mind me marrying him? And Monsieur's happy with that also?

ORGON. Yes, let him sort it out himself. I assume he loves you?

MARIO. Well, I give my consent too.

LISETTE. And me – and I thank all of you.

ORGON. Wait – there's just one condition to add, so I can't be blamed for what happens, and that's that you should give him some hint as to who you really are.

LISETTE. But if I give him a hint, he'll know the whole story.

ORGON. So? If his heart's been well primed, as you say, surely he'll be able to withstand the shock? I don't think he's the sort of man to be scared off that easily.

LISETTE. Here he comes now, looking for me. Please, if you wouldn't mind leaving me a free hand . . . this is going to be my masterpiece.

ORGON. Fair enough, we'll leave you.

SILVIA. With all my heart.

MARIO. Let's go.

Exeunt all except LISETTE. *Enter* ARLEQUIN.

ARLEQUIN. At last, my queen, I can see you, and I'll never leave you again. I've suffered too long from the lack of your presence, and I thought you were evading mine.

LISETTE. There's a degree of truth in that, sir, I must confess.

ARLEQUIN. What, dearest soul, life-giving elixir of my heart, do you seek my death?

LISETTE. Heavens, no, dear sir, your life is much too precious to me.

ARLEQUIN. Ah, how these words give me strength!

LISETTE. And you must never doubt my love.

ARLEQUIN. Oh, how I wish I could kiss those little words, and pluck them from your lips with mine.

LISETTE. But you were pressing me on the question of our marriage, and my father hadn't given me permission to answer you. Well, I've just spoken to him, and I have his consent to tell you that you can ask him for my hand whenever you wish.

ARLEQUIN. Before I ask him for your hand, allow me to ask it from you – I wish to render it my most gracious thanks for the charity it will show me by its willingness to enter into mine, which is truly unworthy of it.

LISETTE. I have no objections to lending it to you for a moment, on condition that you will keep it forever.

ARLEQUIN. Dear plump and chubby little hand, I accept you without reservation. I'm not in the least perturbed about the honour you will do me – my only concern is what I'll be giving you in return.

LISETTE. You'll be giving me more than I need.

ARLEQUIN. Ah, no, not at all – I'm afraid I can do my sums there better than you.

LISETTE. But I regard your love as a gift from heaven.

ARLEQUIN. Well, the gift it's given you isn't likely to
bankrupt it – it's a rather paltry thing.

LISETTE. Actually, I think it's truly magnificent.

ARLEQUIN. That's only because you can't see it in the
cold light of day.

LISETTE. You wouldn't believe how embarrassing I find
your modesty.

ARLEQUIN. Don't waste your embarrassment on me. I'd
be utterly shameless if I weren't modest.

LISETTE. Really, sir, must I keep telling you that I'm the
one who's honoured by your love?

ARLEQUIN. Oh, God – I hardly know where to put myself!

LISETTE. Once again, sir – I know who I am.

ARLEQUIN. Yes, and I know who I am too, and there isn't
that much to know – as you'll find out when you've
finished. It'll be the devil's own job getting to know me –
you never know what you're going to find at the bottom
of the sack.

LISETTE (*aside*). All this servility just isn't natural. (*Aloud.*)
Why are you telling me this?

ARLEQUIN. We're coming to the nub of the matter now.

LISETTE. What do you mean? You're alarming me. Is it
possible that you're not . . .

ARLEQUIN. Oh, dear – now you're lifting the lid off, with
a vengeance.

LISETTE. What on earth is going on?

ARLEQUIN (*aside*). Now, let's just prepare the ground a
little . . . (*Aloud.*) This love of yours, madame, is he of sound

constitution? Is he strong enough to bear the burdens I am about to lay on him? Is he bothered by poor lodgings? I can only offer him cramped quarters, I'm afraid.

LISETTE. Oh, for goodness' sake, put me out of my misery. In one word – who are you?

ARLEQUIN. I am . . . Haven't you ever seen counterfeit money? Do you know what a false coin is? Well, I'm a bit like that.

LISETTE. Get to the point – what is your name?

ARLEQUIN. My name? (*Aside.*) What am I going to say? If I tell her the truth, she'll go through the roof! Hm, that rhymes.

LISETTE. Well?

ARLEQUIN. Well, there's a bit of a problem there, dear lady. Would you have any particular aversion to a soldier?

LISETTE. What do you mean by a soldier?

ARLEQUIN. You know – an *aide de camp*, a batman, sort of – to a gentleman . . .

LISETTE. A batman? To a gentleman? So it isn't actually Dorante I'm speaking to?

ARLEQUIN. Call him my captain, at a stretch.

LISETTE. And I'll call you a lying wretch!

ARLEQUIN (*aside*). I asked for *that* rhyme!

LISETTE. Look at you, you great ape! Take that!

ARLEQUIN (*aside*). How are the mighty fallen!

LISETTE. And to think I've been begging his pardon for a full hour, wearing myself out, grovelling to this miserable creature!

ARLEQUIN. I'm sorry, dear lady, but if you rate love
    higher than pride, you'll make as much profit out of me
    as any fine gentleman.

LISETTE (*laughing*). Ha, ha, ha, I can't help laughing, no
    matter what. Him and his pride! Well, there's nothing
    else for it. Go on, sir, *my* pride pardons you – you're lucky
    it's in a good mood.

ARLEQUIN. Do you really mean that, kind lady? Oh, how
    my love promises to repay you!

LISETTE. Let's shake hands, Arlequin. I've been
    thoroughly fooled. A gentleman's *aide de camp* is well
    worth milady's *coiffeuse*.

ARLEQUIN. What, milady's maid?

LISETTE. Yes, she's my captain, or whatever the equivalent
    is.

ARLEQUIN. Impostor!

LISETTE. Go ahead, take your revenge.

ARLEQUIN. You cheeky little monkey! And to think I've
    spent the past hour, worrying myself sick about being too
    poor!

LISETTE. Well, let's get down to business. Do you love me?

ARLEQUIN. Good God, yes. Changing your name hasn't
    changed your looks, and you know perfectly well we
    promised to be true to each other, regardless of any
    misapprehensions we might be under.

LISETTE. Right, there's no harm done, then – let's console
    ourselves with that. But let's not give the show away, we
    don't want them to laugh at us. It would appear that your
    master is still in the dark about my mistress. Don't make

him any the wiser, let's just keep things as they are. I think
I hear him coming. Now, sir – your humble servant . . .

ARLEQUIN. And I yours, my lady . . . (*Laughs.*)

Exit LISETTE. *Enter* DORANTE.

DORANTE. Now, then, I see you've just left Orgon's
daughter – have you told her who you really are?

ARLEQUIN. God, yes – the poor child. I found her as
meek and mild as a lamb, she hardly said a word. When
I told her my name was Arlequin, and that I wore a
servant's livery, all she said was, 'Oh, well, my friend,
we've all got our names in this life, we've all got our
clothes, and even if yours didn't cost you anything, it
hasn't stopped you being polite.'

DORANTE. What nonsense is this you're telling me?

ARLEQUIN. So, given the way things are, I'm going to ask
for her hand.

DORANTE. What, she's willing to marry you?

ARLEQUIN. She must be sick, eh?

DORANTE. You're having me on – she doesn't know who
you are.

ARLEQUIN. God almighty, sir, do you want to bet I won't
marry her in my servant's livery? I'll wear my dirty
canvas apron too, if you annoy me. I'll have you know,
sir, that a love like mine isn't easily crushed, and I don't
need your fancy cast-offs to win my point – just give me
my own clothes back, that's all I need.

DORANTE. You crafty devil! This is inconceivable – I can
see I'll have to warn Monsieur Orgon.

ARLEQUIN. Who? Our dear father? Oh, he's such a nice man, isn't he – we've got him eating out of our hand. He's a first-rate human being, the very salt of the earth. You will let me know what he says, won't you.

DORANTE. You must be mad! Have you seen Lisette?

ARLEQUIN. Lisette? No. She may have passed before my eyes, but we gentlemen don't take any notice of chambermaids. I'll leave that kind of thing up to you.

DORANTE. Oh, go away – you're off your head.

ARLEQUIN. Hm, your manners are a little too free these days, but I suppose that's a habit you've got into. Anyway, goodbye – once I'm married, of course, we'll live like equals. Ah, here comes your chambermaid. Good morning, Lisette – allow me to commend my man Bourguignon to you – he's quite a decent chap.

Goes out. Enter SILVIA.

DORANTE (*aside*). How worthy she is to be loved! Why did Mario have to get there ahead of me?

SILVIA. Where have you been, sir? I haven't been able to find you again since I left Mario, to let you know what I said to Monsieur Orgon.

DORANTE. Indeed? I haven't strayed very far. Anyway, what's this about?

SILVIA (*aside*). How cold he is! (*Aloud.*) Well, sir, I told him all about your valet, and cited his lack of scruples as evidence of his worthlessness. I suggested he might at least postpone the marriage, but all to no avail – he didn't even listen to me. And I must warn you, sir, they're already talking of sending for the registrar. I think it's time you revealed your true identity.

DORANTE. That's my intention. I'm going to leave here incognito, after I write a letter to Monsieur Orgon explaining everything.

SILVIA (*aside*). He's leaving? That's not what I wanted.

DORANTE. Don't you approve of my idea?

SILVIA. Well . . . not really.

DORANTE. Given the position I'm in, I can't see any other solution, short of speaking to him myself, and I couldn't bring myself to do that. Besides, I have other reasons for wishing to leave. There's nothing else I can do here.

SILVIA. Since I don't know your reasons, I can neither approve of them, nor argue against them, and it's not my place to ask you what they are.

DORANTE. You might easily guess them, Lisette.

SILVIA. Well, for example, I don't think you care too much for Monsieur Orgon's daughter.

DORANTE. Is that all you can see?

SILVIA. Well, there are a good many other things I might suppose, but I'm not silly, or vain enough to dwell on them.

DORANTE. Nor brave enough to speak of them, since you would have nothing gracious to say to me. Goodbye, Lisette.

SILVIA. Be careful. I have to tell you, I don't think you quite take my meaning.

DORANTE. No, I don't, absolutely. And your explanation wouldn't do me any favours. Just keep it to yourself until I'm gone.

SILVIA. You're honestly leaving?

DORANTE. You seem worried I might change my mind.

SILVIA. It's nice of you to be so understanding.

DORANTE. Well, that was very frank. Goodbye.

He turns to leave.

SILVIA (*aside*). If he leaves, I won't love him any more, and
    I'll never marry him . . . (*She watches him going.*) He's
    stopping, though – he's thinking. He's looking to see if
    I'm watching. I wouldn't dream of calling him back, yet
    it would be very strange if he did leave, after everything
    I've done. Ah, well, that's it, he's going – I haven't as
    much power over him as I thought I had. My brother's a
    clumsy oaf, he's got it all wrong – these couldn't-care-less
    people ruin everything. I've taken it too far, it seems, and
    this is how it's turned out. No, wait – Dorante has
    reappeared, I think he's coming back. Ignore what I've
    just said, I still love him . . . Now let's pretend I'm
    leaving, so he'll have to stop me. Our reconciliation really
    ought to cost him something.

DORANTE (*stopping her*). Wait, please – I've something else
    to say to you.

SILVIA. To me, sir?

DORANTE. Yes, I'm finding it hard to leave without
    having convinced you that I'm not wrong to do so.

SILVIA. Oh, really, sir, what's the point of trying to justify
    yourself to me? It's not worth your trouble, I'm only a
    servant, after all, as you've made me very well aware.

DORANTE. Me, Lisette? Have you anything to complain
    about, when you can see me going my way without
    saying a word?

SILVIA. Huh, I could say a few things about that, if I really felt like it.

DORANTE. Well, go on, say them – I'd like nothing better than to be wrong. But what am I saying? Mario loves you.

SILVIA. That's true.

DORANTE. And you're not unmoved by his love. I could see that by how keen you were to get rid of me a moment ago. So you certainly couldn't love me.

SILVIA. Not unmoved by his love? Who told you that? And I couldn't love you? How do you know? You're jumping to conclusions.

DORANTE. Very well, Lisette – by everything I hold most dear in the world, teach me the truth of the matter, I beg you.

SILVIA. Teach a man who is about to leave?

DORANTE. I'm not leaving.

SILVIA. Then leave me alone, and if you love me, stop interrogating me. The only thing you're afraid of is my indifference, and you're quite happy for me to say nothing. What do you care about my feelings?

DORANTE. What do I care, Lisette? Are you still in any doubt that I adore you?

SILVIA. No, and you repeat it so often that I believe you. But why do you keep trying to convince me of it? What do you want me to do with a thought like that, sir? Look, I'll be absolutely frank with you. You love me, yes, but your love isn't a serious thing for you. You have plenty of distractions to help you dispose of it – the great distance between us; the thousands of young women you're likely to encounter on your travels; their willingness to prove you susceptible to their charms; the various amusements open to a man in your position – all these things will soon erase this love you're so relentlessly pleading to me, you'll perhaps even laugh about it as you leave here, and you'll be right to do so. But for my part, sir, if I remember it, as I fear I shall – if I've been smitten, what relief is there for me, from the hurt done to my feelings? Who will console me for the loss of you? Whom do you wish my heart to put in your place? Do you realise that if I loved you, nothing in this world, however important, would ever again move me? Think of the state I would be left in. Please be so kind as to conceal your love from me. Speaking to you as I am now, I would be reluctant to tell you I loved you. In your present mood, any such admission of my feelings might put your reason at risk, and you can see I'm also concealing them.

DORANTE. Oh, my dearest Lisette, what is this I hear? Your words burn into my very soul, I adore you, I respect you – there is neither rank, nor birth, nor fortune, that does not vanish from sight before a heart like yours. I would be deeply ashamed if my pride still held out against you, and my heart and hand now belong to you.

SILVIA. And in truth, sir, if I were to accept them, would you not deserve it? Wouldn't it be rather ungracious of me to conceal my pleasure at your offer? How long do you think that could last?

DORANTE. So you do love me?

SILVIA. No, no – and if you ask me that again, it'll be the worse for you.

DORANTE. Your threats don't frighten me.

SILVIA. What about Mario – have you forgotten him?

DORANTE. No, Lisette. Mario no longer alarms me. You obviously don't love him, you can't deceive me, your heart is true, and you're not immune to my charms. The sheer joy I now feel has silenced all my doubts – I am absolutely certain, and there's nothing you can do to remove that certainty.

SILVIA. Oh, I wouldn't even attempt to. Keep it, and let's see what you do with it.

DORANTE. Will you not consent to be mine?

SILVIA. What, you would marry me in spite of who you are, in spite of a father's wrath, in spite of your fortune?

DORANTE. My father will forgive me the moment he sets eyes on you, my fortune is enough for both of us, and genuine merit is as important as birth. Let's not argue, since I'm never going to change.

SILVIA. He's never going to change! Oh, do you know how enchanting I find you, Dorante?

DORANTE. Don't restrain your love, let it answer . . .

SILVIA. At last, I've reached the end – and you won't ever change, not ever?

DORANTE. No, dearest Lisette, never.

SILVIA. Oh, such love!

Enter ORGON, LISETTE, ARLEQUIN *and* MARIO.

SILVIA. Oh, father, you wanted me to belong to Dorante. Come and see your daughter obeying you with more joy than anyone ever felt.

DORANTE. What's this I hear? You are her father, sir?

SILVIA. Yes, Dorante, we both had the same idea about getting to know one another. Apart from that, I've nothing more to say – you love me, of that I have no doubt, but you in turn can judge my feelings for you, you can judge how much I valued your heart, by the subtlety with which I tried to acquire it.

ORGON. Do you recognise this letter? This is how I learned of your disguise, although she herself only found out from you.

DORANTE. I can't begin to tell you how happy I am, dear lady. But what I find most delightful are the proofs I have already given you of my love.

MARIO. And will Dorante forgive me for making Bourguignon so angry?

DORANTE. He won't forgive you, he'll thank you.

ARLEQUIN (to LISETTE). Be joyful, my lady. You've lost your high rank, but you can't complain, you've still got Arlequin.

LISETTE. Huh, some consolation! You're the only one to profit from this.

ARLEQUIN. Well, I'm certainly not losing by it. Before we got to know one another, your dowry was worth more than you, and now you're worth more than your dowry. Come on, everybody, let's celebrate!

Curtain.